A Father's Love

Words of Wisdom
to Live By

Khoury Porter

Fulton Books
Meadville, PA

Published by Fulton Books 2023

ISBN 979-8-88731-728-1 (paperback)
ISBN 979-8-88731-729-8 (digital)

Printed in the United States of America

Chapter 1

Life Lessons to Live By

The ten points of life

- Honor your creator *God* in heaven.
- Always love yourself.
- Love your mother and father.
- Never forget where you come from.
- Watch the people around you.
- Never underestimate your opponent.
- Watch the things you say.
- Never work for the next man.
- Invest your money.
- Some women are like Samson and Delilah. Do not trust them.

3 types of people

- People who make things happen
- People who watch things happen
- People who say what happened

Hard work

The heights by great men reached and kept were not attained by sudden flight, but they—while their companions slept—kept toiling upward through the night.

The five smarts of life

- Common sense
- Book education
- Street sense
- Maturity
- Life experience

5 attributes of a champion

- Dedication
- Discipline
- Truth
- Vision
- Courage

Foundations for success

- Create good habits.
- Develop a tireless work ethic.
- Focus on what you need to do and not what you want to do.
- Make wise and informed choices.
- Continue to always educate yourself.
- Surround yourself with people who are smarter than you.
- Always look for and take advantage of opportunities that will progress you.
- Stay focused and stay consistent with what you want for yourself.
- Work smart, research your information, and learn to change with adversity.
- Have passion for what you do.

Life lessons for a man

- Always look another man, woman, or child in the eyes.
- Always make sure your actions match your words.
- Never ever sleep with another man's wife.
- Never enter another man's home without him present.
- Never abandon your family or your responsibilities.
- Never put your burdens on the plate of another man.
- Never trust your woman around another man.
- Always give another person the respect they deserve.
- Speak to people with confidence and humility.
- Stand by your morals, integrity, and principals.

Qualities of a leader and successful people

- Stay focused.
- Never stop learning.
- Always sacrifice.
- Stay committed.
- Accept adversity.
- Push yourself past your limitations.
- Stay optimistic.
- Accept change and embrace it.
- Never be satisfied with mediocrity.
- Understand that to be successful, you must be a creature of good habits and work ethic.

Life Lesson 1

Two virtues to live by

- Patience
- Self-control

When I was growing up as a kid, my stepfather used to always tell me, "Khoury, you must always have patience and self-control." As I referred to the diamond and the piece of coal, and like the cobra and the mongoose (stories that you will read later), patience and self-control are crucial to a person's survival, growth, production, and success. Let us look at the definitions of these two words.

Patience: the capacity, habit, or fact of being patient.

Patient: (1) Bearing pains or trials calmly or without complaint. (2) Manifesting forbearance under provocation or strain. (3) Not hasty or impetuous. (4) Steadfast despite opposition, difficulty, or adversity. Being patient will create opportunities for you because of your temperament.

Self-control, according to the dictionary, is the restraint exercised over one's own impulses, emotions, or desires. Let us say this again: the restraint exercised over one's own impulses, emotions, and desires. I personally do not know any person or nor can I think of people I know or have met in my life that have mastered self-control. Self-control will keep you alive, safe, free from harm's way, and in a state of protective peace. Patience and self-control are the only way to live if you want true happiness and success.

Life Lesson 2

Three things not to mess with when dealing with other men

- Money or his ability to make it
- Family
- Wife/woman

Life Lesson 3

Pride: A man's or woman's road to glory or disaster.

Pride: The quality or state of being proud, such as (a) reasonable self-esteem confidence and satisfaction in oneself—self-respect; (b) pleasure that comes from some relationship, association, achievement, or possession that is seen as a source of honor and respect; (c) exaggerated self-esteem—conceit.

In my travels in life, I have seen a lot of people lose their life, get into arguments, break and destroy relationships, and cause people to make poor life choices. Pride, for many reasons, is a beautiful thing to have, but making choices that can put you in a world of grief is never worth it.

Life Lesson 4

Never enter another man's home when he is not there, especially if his wife/woman is home by herself. A man's home is his castle, and everything and everyone in that castle he is willing to protect if they or it becomes or feels threatened.

Life Lesson 5

Relationships are worth more than money. Keep your connections strong with people who have and show true value.

Life Lesson 6

Use me, but do not misuse me. Loyalty, but never stupidity. We all need to fully use our assets that are available to us. Staying true and focused on those who show you the same commitment is a necessity to your development.

Life Lesson 7

In the book of Proverbs, it says the borrower is the slave to the lender. Keep from borrowing money and/or services or favors from other people. Owing someone something that you cannot realistically pay back will be more of headache than a blessing.

Life Lesson 8

If you own a home, you will always need two things: liquid money and a credit card, with at least a $10,000 open-credit limit. Having these two resources will enable you to make home repairs and most minor improvements.

Life Lesson 9

Never trust anyone based solely on their actions. Every action will usually follow a verbal expression from someone first, and their history or reputation will usually give you your answer about their character.

Life Lesson 10

Four credit cards you should own

- American Express
- Visa
- Mastercard
- Discover

You should only use cards that have a point-giveback system. You do not need more than a $10,000 credit limit; anything more than that is an unneeded and unnecessary line of credit. Keep your credit score between 750–850 on the FICO system and 800–900 on the Vantage platform. Always pay your debts on time or early, and make at least the minimum payment.

Life Lesson 11

Things to avoid that create bad habits

- Narcotic drug use
- Alcohol consumption
- Gambling
- Friends and family who take from you but are never willing to give back or help you out in return

Life Lesson 12

When it comes to dating women and to marriage, you're only cute and good-looking in high school. What I am saying is that a man's value to his woman, wife, or girlfriend increases with what he can provide to her. Being cute, good-looking, or attractive may get the woman of your dreams, but it will not keep her.

Life Lesson 13

As a man, when you have a family, you are responsible for the safety, security, and survival of your family at all times. This safety and security include all aspects of those words. This includes the mental and emotional aspects of the people in your care.

Life Lesson 14

If you give your word, stay committed to your word. Honor what rolls out of your mouth and off your tongue.

Life Lesson 15

When eating in a restaurant or enjoying a concert, amusement park, or any other large-person gathering, you take mental notes of all exits and entrances.

Life Lesson 16

Keep to the company of like-minded, positive, and life-progressive people.

Life Lesson 17

Judge people on their character, principles, and morals, or lack thereof.

Life Lesson 18

All information and knowledge are important. Nothing is insignificant or useless when it comes to new information and knowledge.

Life Lesson 19

Research is key to the success of any project or task you encounter on your daily travels. Do your due diligence to find out everything you can before you go into business or start any relationship

Life Lesson 20

Inner city life can create opportunities for business, careers, and youthful entertainment. Suburban communities are best suited for families or for a lifestyle that is more simple and less complex

Life Lesson 21

Learn how to be independent in most things that you choose to get involved in; however, look for those who have more knowledge and experience in the situation you're involved in if you need assistance.

Life Lesson 22

Let your eyes look and focus on what they see. Let your ears hear and listen to what you have heard; and believe what you know, but trust what you can prove. Everything is not always what it seems

Life Lesson 23

Your success is based upon the knowledge on which you obtain. Continue to gain more information and never settle for what you have already acquired.

Life Lesson 24

In the company of a female on a date, make sure you open the door and pull her chair out. When you are walking on the sidewalk, position yourself closest to the street.

Life Lesson 25

Always remember you are a reflection of your father and mother. Never tarnish the legacy of the bloodlines that you come from.

Life Lesson 26

Working hard in life is an incredibly old cliché. Hard, honest work has never killed or hurt anyone in theory. However, smart work is the concept you should focus on more. Why stress yourself with a career or everyday task that you totally hate that causes spiritual, physical, and mental pain?

Life Lesson 27

Always remember to have emergency cash in your home in a secret area that only you, and then at some point your wife or other family member, knows about.

Life Lesson 28

Make sure you keep and have a reliable vehicle.

Life Lesson 29

Not all people you encounter will be your friend. Some people will appear to be assets when, in fact, they are a liability.

Life Lesson 30

Stay focused in the ways of the martial arts and firearms training. Never be a victim of anyone due to the lack of training and discipline you as a man should always possess

Life Lesson 31

Learn how to cook the most basic meals to feed yourself or your loved ones.

Life Lesson 32

Your life success is determined by your consistency and output.

Life Lesson 33

Do not fall for the trickery of laziness or complacency.

Four topics to avoid talking about in public with non-educated and uninformed people

- Race (ethnicity)
- Sex (sexual orientation)
- Politics
- Religion

These four topics have caused more issues among people since the beginning of time. Each human being has a strong sense of pride and conviction when it comes to these topics. It may take a person a lifetime before they are mature enough to discuss these segments in a controlled, intelligent, and unbiased manner. Stay clear of these four if you are not prepared to go to war. Do not let my last statement go over your head.

The most important life lesson is to make sure you understand the lesson you have just learned.

Chapter 2

Let's Get to the Money

Where to put your money

- Stocks
- Mutual funds
- Bonds
- CDs
- Money-market accounts
- Variable annuities
- Real estate
- Franchises
- Business investment groups
- Life insurance
- Swiss bank accounts and Cayman Island banks
- Foreign currency and investments
- Credit unions
- Collectibles and memorabilia
- Jewelry—assets
- Antiques—assets
- Fine art—assets
- Classic automobiles—assets
- Saving accounts
- Service and good businesses—supermarkets, laundromats, restaurants, bars, etc.

Three types of money

- *Savings*—money used for long-term goals, emergencies, or retirement.
- *Spending*—money used for bills and everyday expenses. This money is used for what you need and want.
- *Investment*—Money used for the sole purpose of making profit for your personal wealth. This money works for you. These funds should create residual income for you.

Money Personalities

Biz kid

- Can spend, invest, and save money properly
- Smart with money
- Have entrepreneurial tendencies

Money star

- Loves to show off
- Buys the latest and greatest
- Very materialistic

Penny-wise, pound-foolish

- Loves to save
- Very cost-conscious
- Buys things because it is cheap or because they have a coupon

Oblivious

- Does not understand the concept of money
- Makes random and impulsive purchases
- Does not respect the process of how money is earned

Don't be a credit felon

Credit—the ability of a customer to obtain goods or services before payment based on the trust that a payment will be made in the future.

Creditworthiness—a valuation performed by lenders that determines the possibility a borrower may default on his/her obligations. It considers factors, such as repayment history and credit score.

Credit score—a number assigned to a person that indicates to lenders their capacity to repay a loan.

FICO versus VantageScore (Five Differences)

History. The Fair Isaac Corporation introduced its FICO scoring system in 1989. In 2006 a joint venture between Experian, Equifax, and TransUnion created the VantageScore.

Difference in scoring models

- FICO bases its scoring model on credit reports from millions of consumers at once.
- VantageScore uses a combined set of consumer credit files from the same three credit bureaus to produce a single formula.

Variance in scoring requirements

- If you do not have a long history of credit, VantageScore is the score you want to monitor.
- FICO needs at least six months of credit history and at least one account reported to a CRA to give you a FICO score.

Significance of late payments

- FICO treats all late payments the same.
- VantageScore judges them differently.
- VantageScore penalizes late mortgage payments more harshly than other types of credit.
- If you have had late payments on your mortgage, you might have a higher FICO than VantageScore.

Impact of credit inquiries

- VantageScore and FICO both penalize consumers who have multiple hard inquiries in a short period of time.
- VantageScore and FICO both do deduplication.
- FICO uses a forty-five-day span to deduplicate your inquiries.
- VantageScore limits its focus to fourteen days.
- VantageScore also looks at hard inquiries for all types of credit, including credit cards.
- FICO considers only mortgage, auto, and student loans.

Influence of low balance collections

- FICO ignores all collections where the original balance was under $100. It also does not count collections you have paid off.
- VantageScore ignores only paid collection accounts, regardless of the original balance amount.

How to keep your credit high

- Avoid late payments.
- Keep your credit balances low. Keep the balance at 30 percent or less.
- Apply for new credit only when you must.

Digital Investments

Cryptocurrency—a decentralized digital money designed to be used over the internet.

Most popular cryptocurrencies

- Bitcoin
- Ethereum
- Bitcoin Cash
- Litecoin
- Tezos
- EOS
- Zcash
- Ripple
- Iota
- Tether

- Crypto makes it possible to transfer value online without the need for a go-between, like a bank or payment processor, allowing value to transfer globally, near instantly, 24-7, for low fees.
- Cryptocurrencies are usually not issued or controlled by any government or other central authority. They are managed by peer-to-peer networks of computers running free, open-source software.
- Cryptocurrencies are secured by a technology called a blockchain. A blockchain is like a bank's balance sheet or ledger. Each currency has its own blockchain, which is an ongoing, constantly reverified record of every single transaction ever made using that currency.
- Unlike a bank's ledger, a crypto blockchain is distributed across participants of the digital currency's entire network.
- If you own cryptocurrency, you do not own anything tangible. What you own is a key that allows you to move a record or a unit of measure from one person to another without a trusted third party.

Crypto history

- *Bitcoin.* Founded in 2009, it was the first cryptocurrency. Developed by Satoshi Nakamoto, widely believed to be a pseudonym for an individual or group of people whose precise identity remains unknown.
- *Ethereum.* Developed in 2015, it is a blockchain platform with its own cryptocurrency, called Ether.
- *Litecoin.* It uses the same technology of Bitcoin, and it costs about 1/50th to 1/100th of what Bitcoin does (depending on the day).
- *Bitcoin Cash.* Bitcoin Cash is a spin-off Bitcoin, meant to have faster transactions, voted on and implemented by the Bitcoin community.
- *Ripple (XRP).* Tends to have a steady price due to its large supply. It is a popular and speedy alternative to Bitcoin that often is less volatile than other coins toward the top of the crypto list.
- *Iota.* A popular coin with a large supply (meaning there are many MIOTAs out there). It has one of the highest market caps today due to the tech behind it being embraced by companies like Cisco Systems, Volkswagen, and Samsung.
- *Tether.* This coin is meant to reflect the price of the US dollar. If you want a stable coin for temporary use, Tether tends to be a good choice. It is not an investment; it is a place to park your value in crypto when you are in between coins.

NFT

NFT (non-fungible token). NFT is a digital asset that represents real-world objects, like art, music, in-game items and videos. They are bought and sold online, frequently with cryptocurrency, and they are encoded with same underlying software as many cryptos. They are gaining notoriety now because they are becoming an increasingly popular way to buy and sell digital artwork. NFTs are also generally one of a kind, or at least one of an extremely limited runs, and have unique identifying codes. NFTs create digital scarcity. Anyone can view the individual images or even the entire collage of images online for free. An NFT allows the buyer to own the original item. NFTs contain built-in authentication, which serves as proof of ownership. NFTs are different from cryptocurrencies; each has a digital signature that makes it impossible for NFTs to be exchanged for or equal. NFTs exist on a blockchain. They are typically held on the Ethereum blockchain. NFTs also get exclusive ownership rights. They can have only one owner at a time, and their use of blockchain technology makes it easy to verify ownership and transfer tokens between owners. The creator of an NFT can also store specific information in an NFT's metadata. Artist can sign their artwork by including their signature in the file. Artist can sell it (NFT) to the consumer, which also lets them keep more of the profits. In addition, artists can program in royalties, so they will receive a percentage of sales whenever their art is sold to a new owner.

How to buy NFTs

- Digital wallet
- Purchase cryptocurrencies
- Move your currency to your wallet

NFT marketplaces

- *OpenSea.io.* Peer-to-peer platform bills itself a purveyor of "race digital items and collectibles." To get started, all you need to do is create an account to browse NFT collections.
- *Rarible.* Rarible is a democratic, open marketplace that allows artists and creators to issue and sell NFTs. Rari tokens issued on the platform enable holders to weigh in on features like fees and community rules.
- *Foundation.* On this platform, artists must receive "upvotes" or invitation from creators to post their art. The communi-

ty's exclusivity and cost of entry artists must also purchase "gas" to mint NFTs.

Important information

- NFTs are subject to capital gains taxes.
- Cryptocurrencies used to purchase may also be taxed.

How Much Money Do I Keep?

Federal income tax rates (married)

Rates for single people are a little higher but are in the same ballpark.

- 10%—0 to $19,900
- 12%—$19,901 to $81,050
- 22%—$81,051 to $172,750
- 24%—$172,751 to $329,950
- 32%—$329,851 to $418,850
- 35%—$418,851 to $628,300
- 37%—$628,301 or more

NYS tax rate

- 4%—0 to $17,150
- 4.5%—$17,151 to $23,600
- 5.25%—$23,601 to $27,900
- 5.9%—$27,901 to $43,000
- 5.97%—$43,001 to $161,550
- 6.33%—$161,551 to $323,200
- 6.85%—$323,201 to $2,155,350
- 9.65%—$2,155,351 to $5,000,000
- 10.30%—$5,000,001 to $25,000,000
- 10.90%—over $25,000,000

Social Security—6.20%
Medicare—1.45%

- To gain true financial wealth, you must have multiple streams of income. You cannot have one sole stream of income. Diversifying your income portfolio will put you on the right path for financial freedom.
- If you cannot purchase something at least three times, then you cannot afford it. It does not matter if it is a piece of gum or a car. If you do not have the ability to purchase it three times over, then it is out of your budget.
- Develop the habit of saving your money. In these modern times, there are numerous apps that allow you to save and/or invest minimal amounts of money.
- Always remember to always keep liquid cash on you and in your home. Cash is king! The power of the dollar in its physical form goes a long way.

The Power of Passive and Residual Income

Residual income is the amount of money an individual or business has left after paying all expenses.

Personal residual income is any remaining money after an individual pays all housing, food, and other expenses, and pays off debts.

Residual income formula = net income – (equity x cost of equity)

- Net income is earnings after all expenses, costs, interest accrued, depreciation, amortization, and taxes.
- Equity is the total assets, minus the total liabilities, enumerated on the balance sheet.
- Cost of equity is minimum return required on an investment.

Passive income is the accumulation of capital earned by a company with little effort required to get it. In personal finance, passive income refers to income generated from a side business or investment.

Types of residual income

- Real estate investing
- Stocks
- Bonds. Bonds help you have an ownership stake in loans taken out by companies and governments. Investors receive fixed-rate interest payments about twice a year. Once a loan matures, then you can reinvest in other bonds to have consistent cash flow coming in and out of the business.
- Royalties is an amount of money that goes to the owner of a product or patent by those using that product or patent on an ongoing or one-use basis. It could be assets, intellectual property, resources, or copyrighted material.

Life Lesson 34

I have heard, witnessed, read, and have experienced people in my lifetime equate a person's wealth or lack thereof as a measuring stick for that person's character, values, and morals. Large amounts of money or the net worth of a person is not what matters. The actions a person takes when they acquire wealth and good financial fortune is what will define their true character and spirit. I heard of a lot of rich people who trafficked young women and children for sexual fantasies or paid off politicians to gain favor in their communities; school board officials doing the wrong thing for the right financial compensation; mother's and father's taking hush money even though they knew a pedophile abused their children. Even the biggest religious organizations have paid people off to cleanse away the wrong doings of their clergy and spiritual leaders. Money does not define a person. It enhances a person for the good or evil person they may be by ten times. Man makes the money; money does not make the man.

Keep your pockets full by keeping your heart pure and your mind and spirit open and honest.

> But they that will be rich fall into temptation and a snare, and into many foolish and hurtful lusts, which drown men in destruction and perdition. For the love of money is the root of all evil. (1 Timothy 6:9–10)

Chapter 3

The Power of Our People

African American, Afro Caribbean, and Black people in business

Kenneth Chenault

- The former CEO and COO of American Express 1997–2018.
- He is the third African American to serve as a CEO of a Fortune 500 company.
- He joined Amex in 1981 and rose through the ranks.
- He has served on executive boards for the following companies: (a) IBM, (b) Procter & Gamble, (c) Airbnb, (d) Facebook, (e) Berkshire Hathaway, (f) NCAA Board of Governors.
- In 2021 he was featured in *Time* magazine's Time 100, the annual list of the one hundred most influential *people* in the world.

Byron Allen

- Founder and CEO of Entertainment Studios.
- He owns the Weather Channel.
- In 2019 his company helped purchase Fox Sports networks.
- His TV show, *Kickin' It: With Byron Allen*, started in 1992 and ran for thirteen seasons.
- 2021–2022 net worth $450 million.

Marvin Ellison

- CEO of Lowes Corporation.
- Est. net worth thirty million dollars.
- Annual salary $1.45 million; with bonuses, it can range between $11–$15 million.

Kenneth Frazier

- Former CEO of Merck.
- He made $60,192,225 (2014–2016).
- His net worth is estimated in the hundreds of millions of dollars.

Rene F. Jones

- CEO of M&T Bank.
- Annual salary of five million dollars.
- Estimated net worth of fifteen million dollars.

Inventions by African Americans that impacted the world

- Laser eye surgery—Patricia Bath, 1981
- Air-conditioning unit—Frederick M. Jones, 1949
- Almanac—Benjamin Banneker, 1791
- Baby buggy (stroller)—William H. Richardson, 1889
- Blood plasma bag—Charles Drew, 1945
- Clothes dryer—George T. Sampson, 1971
- Doorknob and doorstop—Osbourn Dorsey, 1878
- Electric lamp Bulb—Lewis Latimer, 1882
- Elevator—Alexander Miles, 1867
- Fire extinguisher—Thomas Marshall, 1872
- Folding chair—Nathaniel Alexander, 1911
- Golf Tee—George T. Grant, 1899
- Guitar—Robert F. Fleming Jr., 1886
- Ironing board—Sarah Boone, 1887

- Lawn sprinkler—John H. Smith, 1897
- Lock—Washington A. Martin, 1893
- Lubricating cup—Elijah McCoy, 1895
- Mailbox—Paul Downing, 1891
- Peanut butter—George W. Carver, 1896
- Pencil sharpener—John Love, 1897
- Spark plug—Edmond Berger, 1839
- Stethoscope—Thomas A. Carrington, 1876
- Straightening comb—Madam CJ Walker, 1905
- Street sweeper—Charles B. Brooks, 1890
- Thermostat control—Fredrick M. Jones, 1960
- Traffic light—Garrett Morgan, 1923
- Railway signal—A. B. Blackburn, 1888
- Lawn mower—J. A. Burr, 1899
- Horseshoe—O. E. Brown, 1899
- Record player arm—Joseph H. Dick, 1819

The richest man in the history of the world: Mansa Musa

Born in AD 1280, Mansa Musa came into power in 1312 as the ruler and king of the Mali Empire. The Mali Empire was filled with numerous resources, such as salt and gold.

A devout Muslim man, he made the pilgrimage to Mecca in accordance with his faith. He made the four-thousand-mile journey with sixty thousand men, which included the entire royal court, soldiers, and twelve thousand slaves. On his journey, he willfully handed out pieces of gold to the impoverished people his caravan encountered on their travels. Not to mention each person who traveled with him—from soldier to slave—wore gold jewelry and Persian silk; even the camels had gold fixed to them. His generosity of passing out gold to the poor caused Egypt to go into a financial crisis that lasted twelve years. The reason for Egypt's economic plummet was due to gold losing its value during Mansa Musa's charitable donations to the poor and disenfranchised.

King Musa attempted to fix Egypt's economic woes by borrowing gold from Egypt at high interest rates. It is the only time in world history that one man controlled the entire gold industry and pricing. During his rule, he controlled twenty-four different cities, and he built schools, libraries, and mosques. As of September 2022, according to Forbes, Elon Musk is the wealthiest person on the planet Earth, with a net worth of $241 billion. Jeff Bezos of Amazon fame is valued at $151 billion. Indian industrialist Gautam Adani is valued at $141 billion, and Microsoft founder, Bill Gates, is worth $114 billion dollars respectfully.

No one knows how much Mansa Musa's actual worth is. However, some internet theorists have estimated King Musa's worth at a minimum four hundred billion dollars. This number is an estimate and most modern-day financial analyst feel king Musa's worth is much more.

How '64 helped millions

In 1964 President Lyndon B. Johnson, backed by Roy Wilkins and Clarence Mitchell, finished what President John F. Kennedy, Martin Luther King Jr., and Medgar Evers, to name a few, started in the years prior to '64. In 1964 Congress passed Public Law 88-352 (78 Stat. 241). The Civil Rights Act of 1964 prohibits discrimination based on race, color, religion, sex, or national origin. Provisions of this civil rights act forbade discrimination based on sex, as well as race, in hiring, promoting, and firing. The act prohibited discrimination in public accommodations and federally funded programs. It also strengthened the enforcement of voting rights and the desegregation of schools. The Civil Rights Act of '64 has helped millions of American lives move into levels of progression. Every American citizen and all other people who live, work, worship, raise families, and enjoy all other liberties of this country have benefited from the suffrage of Black people. Through the struggles, discrimination, bias, death, segregation, pain, suffering, and alienation of Black people in this country, all human beings who can take in the comforts and luxuries of feeling safe in their communities and everyday lives here in America should always feel grateful and indebted to their Black brothers and sisters. Fight the power.

The roar of the panther

The Black Panther Party for Self-Defense was started in Oakland California in 1966 by Huey P. Newton and Bobby Seale. The party was started to combat police brutality in the Black community in the bay area. Throughout the party's existence, programs like free health clinics, free breakfast programs, tuberculosis testing, legal aid, free-shoe program, ambulance program, transportation assistance, and grocery delivery were started. The party had many colorful members and influential leaders in the inner-city Black communities of America. The free breakfast program had a major influence on the USDA's free breakfast efforts, which in turn forced the hand of the American government to institute the free national breakfast program, which affects 14.57 million American children each year. The party's actions on May 2, 1967, would forever change the landscape in the aspect of gun control and its future legislative position in this country. Thirty Black Panther party members armed with rifles and shotguns entered the California State Building in protest of gun-control bills specifically aimed at Americans bearing firearms in an open-carry fashion. The panthers were considered the most dangerous group to American national security by J. Edgar Hoover and the FBI in 1969. Even though the party was dismantled and eventually died out, the legacy of what they stood for should be a model for all communities that believe in the upliftment of the people they intertwine with.

African American and Afro Caribbean influence on American popular culture

- Hip-hop music and culture
- Jazz music
- Rhythm and blues music
- Rock and roll music
- Gospel music
- Jack Daniels whiskey (Jack Daniels was taught by Nathan "Nearest" Green to be an alcohol distiller)
- The moonwalk dance move

- The high five hand gesture
- The American cowboy (not to be confused with the outlaw criminals of America's Wild West culture)
- The buffalo soldiers
- The Afro hairstyle
- The hustle and electric slide dances
- Tap and jazz style of dance
- The perm hairstyle
- Urban-based American slang
- The beef patty
- Rice
- Capitalism
- The concept of factories
- Laws concerning human rights and overall discrimination
- The redlining laws
- Gentrification
- Numerous state and federal laws
- Every invention listed above that changed the landscape of human beings in this country and abroad that help navigate everyday life

Thank God for capitalism, or should we?

Capitalism—an economic system characterized by private or corporate ownership of capital goods by investments that are determined by private decision, and by prices, production, and the distribution of goods that are determined by competition in a free market.

Capitalize—to gain by turning something to an advantage.

Examples of capitalization. The English Royal African Company introduced the franchising concept in 1668 in their efforts to control the now booming slave trade in western Africa. For a 15 percent royalty of the slaveholders' profits, the company would provide their "franchisees" with land, supplies, slaves, military protection, and a final retail market for their slave produced goods.

In the early 1980s and in August 2000, New York City decided to auction and sell lots of land and historical brownstone apartment buildings in Harlem, New York. The city owned most of the property in Harlem at this time. By 1975 NYC owned about 65 percent of the real estate in Manhattan's Black community. The price points for these properties for auction and/or purchase varied from $1.00 to $42,000. Applicants needed to be Harlem residents in some cases and have other income-based criteria to enter the lotteries, auctions, and sales of these historical NYC sites. As of August 2022, a Harlem brownstone was sold for $6.9 million dollars. Go figure.

Henrietta Lacks

Born Loretta Pleasant on August 1, 1920, in Roanoke, Virginia, Henrietta's death from cervical cancer would change the landscape of the medical research industry forever. The harvesting of Mrs. Lacks's cells for cancer and medical research was done without her consent during a biopsy in 1951. No one from the Lacks family, or anyone else in the known free world for that matter, had a clue that Henrietta's cells were extracted from her during this procedure. Mrs. Lacks had a unique cell structure; this cell uniqueness allowed her cells to live much longer than the average human cell. This gave George Otto Gey, the first researcher to study Henrietta's cells, the opportunity to create what is known today in the medical field as HeLa cells. Cancer, AIDS, radiation and toxic substances, gene mapping, and many other scientific and medical advancements, have been made due to Mrs. Lack's genetic gift.

What is true power?

As Ben Parker once told his nephew Peter Parker, aka the amazing Spider-Man, "With great power comes great responsibility," we as a human species—and as black, brown, red, yellow, white, and every color of the spectrum of the male kind—we must do our due diligence to understand the nature of our power as men, boys, and males. As being a Black man in America raising two Black bi-ethnic sons, I have an unprecedent duty to both my young men to make sure they understand their power and significance to the culture and development of our people. As for the countless other males who may or may not read this book who are not African American, Afro Caribbean, or African, you as a young, old, adolescent, or plain ole regular man, have a duty to protect, provide, educate, care, uphold, and nourish your families and communities.

Who and what Black men are to the human existence and history, past and present

- Mansa Musa—king of Mali Empire and the richest human being in history.
- Ramesses II—the pharaoh of historical and biblical fame who ruled over the ancient nation of Kemet (Egypt) and the Hebrews that Moses led from his rule.
- Hannibal—the North African Muslim general who conquered most of Southern Europe.
- Shaka Zulu—South African king who made numerous militaristic advancements in hand-to-hand combat in the continent of Africa. His buffalo-horns style of warfare defeated the rifle toting British in 1879.
- Nelson Mandela—South African freedom fighter and civil rights activist who served twenty-seven years in prison and then came out of his imprisonment to become the president of the country.
- Martin Luther King Jr.—American civil rights leader of the 1960s who helped change the landscape of the American Black man, woman, and child.
- Malcom X—American civil rights leader of the 1960s that was once a career criminal and then rose to the top of the nation of Islam and inspired numerous generations of Black men in the concept of Black nationalism.
- Huey P. Newton and Bobby Seale—the cofounders of the Black Panther Party. At the height of the party, they were an estimated two thousand members nationwide.
- Josiah Henson helped establish a Black community in what is now Ontario, Canada. He helped slaves escape slavery and led them up into Canada to freedom. He is the char-

acter used by Harriet Beecher Stowe for her novel *Uncle Tom's Cabin*. In no way was Josiah Henson like the character depicted in Stowe's novel.

- Barack Obama—the forty-fourth president of the United States of America. This half-Kenyan, half-Caucasian man and former State of Illinois US senator became the first man of color in the modern era to become the commander-in-chief of the United States.

- Muhammad Ali—three-time heavyweight champion of the world, 1960 gold medalist, civil rights advocate, and a world ambassador of goodwill.

- Walter Lincoln Hawkins—chemical engineer who developed the polymer that is used to wrap telephone wires. He owns eighteen US patents and 129 foreign patents.

- Dr. Joseph Waters—material scientist for Intel corporation, and he has a PhD in material science from the University of Alabama.

- Dr. Rupert N. Green—internal medicine general practitioner physician. During World War 2, he was a lab assistant for the Manhattan Project, and he served as a physician in the United States Army during the war.

There are countless other men of color in the Black community that contributed to all different genres of life. The list far surpasses the names of the men I previously listed. I purposely did not list athletes or entertainers in a large abundance since we all know who they are already; however, do we know the ones who have made strides in the health care, business, science, and education fields? We must do better when it comes to acknowledging and giving flowers of praise and admiration for those who do not dunk or throw a ball or spit a hot sixteen-bar rap verse.

A man makes a difference

The male role model and presence is too important in the role of society, family, and community. When I look back into my past, I find myself asking the question of how different I would have been if I had more men in my community like Dr. Green (my stepfather and the man who raised me), or a David Kern (father-in-law), or a Ramon Rivera (my brother, martial arts instructor, mentor, and the man who saved my life). These men I have just named made the biggest impacts on my life as an adult.

As a child, I had Everett and Winston Waters and their father, Donald Waters (my cousins and uncle), to help shape my mind and spirit as a young boy and into a man. In the Edenwald projects of the northeast Bronx, there was Jaime and his crew, keeping a watchful and protective eye on me to make sure the drug wars of the 1980s in my projects did not make me its victim. Lou Madison made sure I played basketball in Culver Street Park in southside Yonkers and stayed off the streets and took sports as a positive path to success in life. Dean, the barber, would tell me every time he saw me in the shop to stay out of the street life and use my head and that I was better than the life I was choosing at that time. Jim Bostic at the Nepperhan Community Center inspired and gave me the opportunity to speak and mentor youth in the city of Yonkers who were caught in the traps of gangs, violence, and drugs like I was as a young man. John "Jazz" Earl gave me and my music team a place to record our music and try to make that rap dream I had come true.

All these men and some I cannot remember tried their best to give me guidance, game, tough and nurturing love at different intervals of my life. The male figure is more than just the provider, the protector, or the roughest toughest dude in your hood, community, place of work, or your high school. This male figure is and should be a light house of hope, integrity, morals, honor, and a helping hand while you navigate this thing we call life.

> Pain and negativity that is not transformed
> inside of you gets transferred from you on to
> other people. (Pastor Greg Doll)

Chapter 4

What Is Business and Success?

Words to live by to be successful

- *Sacrifice*—destruction or surrender of something for the sake of something else; something given up or lost.
- *Commitment*—an agreement or pledge to do something in the future.
- *Focus*—a center of activity, attraction, or attention; a point of concentration; a directed attention; a state or condition permitting clear perception or understanding.
- *Discipline*—orderly or prescribed conduct or pattern of behavior; self-control; training that corrects, molds, or perfects the mental faculties or moral character; to train or develop by instruction and exercise, especially in self-control.
- *Habit*—an acquired mode of behavior that has become or completely involuntary; a behavior pattern acquired by frequent repetition or physiological exposure that shows itself in regularity or increased facility of performance.

Two types of people in small business

- *Self-employed*—self-employed people work solely for themselves and contract directly with their clients.
- *Business owner*—the founder or creator of a business who owns the business and reaps the financial benefits of the

business by managing and directing the activities of the business.

Types of businesses

- *Sole proprietorship.* A sole proprietorship is an unincorporated company that is owned by one individual only. It offers the least amount of financial and legal protection for the owner. Sole proprietorships do not create a separate legal identity for the business. The owner of the business shares the same identity as the company. The owner is fully liable for any all liabilities incurred by the company. There are also tax benefits as income is considered the owner's personal income and therefore only taxed once.
- *Partnership.* A partnership is a business owned by two or more people. Like sole proprietorships, partnerships can take advantage of flow through taxation.
- *General partnership.* There is unlimited liability for every partner. Each partner is responsible for every other partner's actions.
- *Limited partnership.* This type of partnership has at least one general partner. The general partner takes on unlimited liability for the partnership and manages the operations of the company. Limited partners only take on as much liability as their financial stake in the business. Limited partners are not involved in management decisions and do not have any direct control over the company.
- *Limited liability partnership.* Partners in LLPs are not personally responsible for the actions of the other partners or the debts of the business. Not all businesses can be LLPs. This type of business is often restricted to certain professions such as lawyers or accountants.
- *Limited liability company.* LLCs combine aspects of both partnerships and corporations. They retain the tax benefits of sole proprietorships and the limited liability of corporations. LLCs can choose between different tax treatments.

If the LLC chooses not to be treated as a C corporation, it retains its flow through taxation status. LLCs exists as their own legal entity.

- *Corporations.* Corporations are a separate entity created by shareholders. Articles of incorporation must be drafted, which include information such as the number of shares to be issued, the name and location of the business, and the purpose of the business. Corporations exist as a legally separate entity.
  a) C corporation is taxed as a business entity and owners receive profits that are then also taxed individually.
  b) S corporation. This corporation may only have one hundred shareholders. S corps are pass-through entities like partnerships, so profits are not taxed twice.
  c) Nonprofit corporation. Often used by charitable organizations, nonprofit corporations are tax-exempt.

Men who followed their own path to success

Warren Buffet

- Started playing with the stock market at age eleven.
- In high school, he earned $50 per week with a pinball business that he started.
- In the 1960s he bought 5 percent of American Express' stock despite the company's near-bankrupt state.
- 2022 net worth: $111.8 billion.

Sam Walton

- Started as JCPenney manager out of college.
- Opened his own franchise in 1945 called Ben Franklin.
- Created the concept of the discount store which primarily focused on small-town markets.

- By his death in 1992, his small-town discount store concept had 1,735 Walmarts, 212 Sam's Clubs, 13 supercenters, 380,000 employees, and $50 billion in annual sales.
- 1992 net worth: $22 billion.

Michael Dell

- He started selling refurbished computers while he was in college.
- He sold the computers door to door.
- All the computers he refurbished himself.
- He made $180,000 from the computer sales, dropped out of college, and started Dell computers.

William Henry Gates III, aka Bill Gates

- Wrote his first software program at thirteen.
- In high school, he formed the company Traf-O-Data, a company that sold traffic-counting systems.
- Left Harvard University in his junior year to start Microsoft with his friend Paul G. Allen.
- 2022 net worth: $125 billion.

Books to read in your life for your life's success

- *The Greatest Salesman in the World*
- *The Go-Giver*
- *Think and Grow Rich*
- *Rich Dad Poor Dad*
- *Who Moved My Cheese?*
- *The 48 Laws of Power*
- *Chess Not Checkers*
- *The Autobiography of Malcolm X*
- *How To Win Friends and Influence People*
- *Men Are from Mars, Women Are from Venus*
- *Millionaire Success Habits*

- *The Bible (the New Living Translation)*
- *Priceless: Straight-Shooting, No Frills Financial Wisdom*
- *From Babylon to Timbuktu*
- *Dirty Little Secrets: About Black History, Its Heroes, and Other Troublemakers*
- *The New World Order*
- *Behold A Pale Horse*
- *The Art of War*

What it means to be a professional

- Education gives you knowledge and insight.
- Training provides a means of developing skills.
- Experience expands upon and refines those skills and helps to develop one's abilities.
- Attitude ties knowledge, skills, and abilities.

What do I need to start my own business?

- A solid idea or concept to build upon
- A product or service
- A business plan
- Three years' savings of your current bills
- 650-plus credit score
- A company structure (LLC, corporation, partnership)

Three stages of business

- *Red*—the business is bleeding, and it is causing you to lose money and forcing you into having to pay out of your own pocket for the business' expenses.
- *Black*—the business is in a state of financial balance. It is not losing money nor is it making a profit.
- *Green*—the business is creating profitable revenue.

Your network is your net worth

Five lessons on building stronger networks

1. Weak ties will improve your chances of success. Collaborate and build with people outside your personal circle.
2. Networking isn't about selling a specific product or service.
3. Successful relationships are built on mutual trust.
4. Personalize your approach for everyone.
5. Your network exists outside of work.

Businesses that are recession and pandemic proof

- Supermarkets
- Grocery store
- Pharmacy
- Garbage and rubbish removal
- Delivery services (Instacart, GrubHub, etc.)
- Medical clinics
- Mortuary
- Uber and Lyft and taxi services
- Laundromat
- Security (armed and unarmed)
- Ambulette services
- Visiting nurse and home health-care services
- Farm
- Online services and activities
- Logistics (trucking services and delivery, like FedEx, UPS, etc.)
- Haircare services (barber and hairstylist)
- Mobile food vendor

What causes failure in life and business

Failure—a state of inability to perform a normal function; a fracturing or giving way under stress; lack of success; a falling short

Causes of failure in business

1. Not enough demand
2. Lack of cash or a cash reserve, aka a cash cushion
3. Dysfunctional team
4. Established competition
5. Pricing issues (too low or too high or not competitive with your competitors)

Businesses with the lowest failure rates

1. Healthcare and social assistance—15 percent fail in the first year, 25 percent fail in the second year, and 40 percent fail in the fifth year.

Businesses with the highest failure rate

2. Construction industry—25 percent in the first year.
3. Transportation industry—25 percent in the first year.
4. Both industries fail in the second year 35 percent of the time and by 60 percent by year five.

Business failure percentages

*   Arts, entertainment, and recreation—11.6%
*   Real estate, rental, and leasing—12%
*   Food service industry (including restaurants)—15%
*   Finance and insurance—16.4%
*   Professional, scientific, and technical services—19.4%

Causes of failure in life

*   Lack of direction
*   Lack of good habits
*   Making consistent wrong choices

- Refusing to continue to learn new and innovative things
- Letting failure freeze them from moving onward

How do we succeed in business?

- Having a sense for what your customers want and need
- Having the ability to change with your demographics
- Proper location (brick and mortar)
- Having a good marketing and advertising strategy
- Staying focused and consistent with good habits

How so we succeed in life?

- Setting goals
- Staying focused on completing your goals
- Being willing to do more than the average person
- Staying focused and consistent with good habits
- Making consistent good choices
- Giving more than what's expected in any situation
- Staying genuine, true, and honest with yourself always
- Learning to except the failure as well as the prosperity

Defining success for men and the male species

From the time I was a little boy, everything I did was based around some accomplishment that had to do with a sport, being with a pretty girl, or beating and standing up to the bully. As you grow from a young boy into an adolescent, you are then told verbally and nonverbally to reach for things that have tangible value to the status of your manhood. The success of accomplishing your goals releases dopamine from your brain and sets the mental and spiritual mood for us to feel like a real man. But what is truly success to my species? Is it having a beautiful car and the beautiful woman? Is it being at the top of the corporate ladder or being a general in the armed forces? What is success for a man in any society? Is it financial freedom that enables to buy the luxury car to show off to all his friends and enemies? The degree from community college or the experience of having Harvard on your résumé may just be what you need. For me, success as a man is knowing that I've made myself proud, keeping my daily actions and reputation clean from dishonorable actions, trying my best at all costs to be a good husband, role model, father, and mentor on a day-to-day basis for all those who look upon me for that guiding light.

> Success is most often achieved by those who don't know that failure is inevitable. (Coco Chanel)

> Relationships are worth more than money. (Kevin "NFL" Reavis)

> Network until there is no more space left in your net. (Khoury R. Porter)

> Life is like chess; make the right moves and decisions and you'll win the game. (Khoury R. Porter)

Chapter 5

Parables and Metaphors

What makes you a diamond

It takes a piece of coal deep inside the earth's surface thousands and millions of years under enormous and intense levels of pressure, heat, and toxic gasses to have the ability to become a rough diamond. Once the diamond is formed, it must be mined and then looked at by a diamond cutter to evaluate it, to decide what shape it will become. If you can't become the diamond of your choice and you remain the original piece of coal, you still have purpose in life. Coal is used to produce cement, carbon fibers and foams, medicines, and to heat people's homes. Not to mention you can make great steaks and burgers on a coal-powered grill at your local family BBQ. People don't understand the power of their purpose. Pressure can make us into a beautiful work of art or a plain ole piece of BBQ home-heating coal. Even the diamond still isn't perfect; it must be cut, shaped, and polished. Hard lives, hard decisions, trials, and tribulations are a part of our universe no matter what we or the life we live choose for us to be. Decide for yourself how pressure will shape and mold you.

The cobra and the mongoose

In life, perception is a powerful concept. We all project an image to our peers, family, colleagues, and friends that they may or may not understand. The great king cobra is the world's longest venomous snake. It can reach a length of nineteen feet in ideal habitat situations. It contains a potent neurotoxic venom that can kill a human within thirty minutes after being bitten. The Indian grey mongoose of Southeast Asia is known to have the ability to combat and hunt venomous snakes. Stiff fur, hypersensitive reflexes, and internal natural receptors to resist snake venom give them the abilities to hunt snakes. In this case, you have two predators that must encounter each other daily; two hunters who, when they meet, must decide who's the hunter and who's the prey. One of these creatures will fight for their survival. The question is, which one is the hunter, and who is truly the prey due to our perception of good and bad? The choice is yours to decide. The cobra or the mongoose?

The lifeboat

There are many different versions of this concept. Garrett Hardin authored an article in 1974 called "The Tragedy of the Commons," in which he describes a lifeboat that could or could not take on swimmers stranded in the ocean. Harden's concept was based upon the world's rich and poor populations. My concept is based on two things of the human condition and experience. The first being self-preservation, and the second principle of patience and self-control. When I was a young child, my stepfather, Dr. Rupert N. Green, used to drill into my head the concept of patience and self-control. For thirty-plus years, he would say, "Son, you must have patience and self-control to be successful." Now, the concept of the lifeboat I use is the concept of you having been displaced from a cruise ship, fishing boat, pontoon etc. You are now in the middle of the ocean, and a lifeboat appears to help save you and one other survivor from your other vessel. Only patience and self-control in this high-pressure situation will allow one of you to get into the boat and then help the other person get into the boat safely as well. Because most people lack the discipline of patience and self-control, they will try to get into the boat first and totally disregard the other person who is in the exact same predicament as themselves. Staying calm and waiting your turn can put you in a much more advantageous position.

The power of choice

I am not a graduate of any college, university, trade, or technical school. I am not a certified specialist in a particular social science or skill. I am a human being, a man, a father, brother, coach, instructor, husband, mentor, and a friend. I have lived my life through trials, tribulations, happiness, grief, and failure. In the years that I lived my life, I have come to understand, recognize, and appreciate that the most powerful thing in a person's existence is the power of choice. Love, hate, fear, anger, greed, religious beliefs, and other feelings or state of being that a person goes into is usually from the choice that they make. Now, some people will say that having a psychological issue or physical disability dictates a person's choice. That may be true in those instances; however, for healthy people who are in normal conditions, their choice is the singular most powerful thing in their life. Your choices will direct you, affect you, neglect, incarcerate, kill you, bless you, or empower you. Choice allows you to stay focused, disciplined, healthy, alive, and well. I know they say love, hate, and hope are the end all; however, the choices we make give us the quality of life that we all want or hate to have. You choose to be loyal, faithful, racist, sexist, or optimistic, and happy. Make the choice to be fruitful and at peace with your life, and everything will blossom from there.

The liar and a thief

The four types of liars

1. Deceitful
2. Duplicitous
3. Delusional
4. Demoralized

Deceitful liars. These people lie to others about facts: skillful liars (people who know how and when to lie), white liars (people who lie for personal gain and do not cause malicious results), habitual liars (people who lie on a consistent basis for no reasons). All these liars fall in this category.

Duplicitous liars. These people lie to others about their values. Duplicitous comes from the Latin word for "twofold" or "double."

Delusional liars. These people lie to themselves.

Demoralized liars. These people lie to themselves about their values.

Thief. A thief is one that steals especially stealthily or secretly.

Which one of these types of people do you trust? One of these people you must pick and trust with your life, your family, your belongings, and your time. Most people are going to say, "I wouldn't trust either one of these types of people." In your life, you will always deal with these two types of people no matter if you like it or not. In my personal experience, you can always trust a thief to do exactly what a thief will do, and that is to steal every time you put him or her in a situation that they feel they need to steal. In the case of a liar, you can never trust a liar with anything but the fact that you can't trust them at all. A liar is the worst kind of person to keep active in your daily life. At the end of the day, a thief is more trustworthy than a liar; however, we must try to remove both from our lives.

Who's riskier, stocks or people?

Stock market statistics, facts, and history

1. In November 2020 total market capitalization reached a record $95 trillion dollars, surpassing pre-coronavirus levels.
2. There are nineteen stock exchanges in the world. These stock exchanges accounted for more than 87 percent of global market capitalization in 2015. NASDAQ and the New York Exchange have more market cap between them than the rest of the exchanges in the world.
3. Middle-class households have lost more than of household equity holdings since 1989.

4. About 10 percent of US households hold international equity.

5. Stock market declines of 5 percent to 10 percent require a month's recovery time.

6. In 2018 the United States represented 40.1 percent of global market capitalization. In 2020 this figure rose to 54.5 percent.

7. Valued at $2.25 trillion, Apple leads the world's corporations in market capitalization.

8. 27.6 percent of the market share is controlled by the information technology sector. Health care is in second place at 13.44 percent, and the communication industry is at fourth place at 10.79 percent market share.

9. More than 80 percent of the stock market is now automated.

10. Since 1903, every day at the New York Stock Exchange, the day starts with the ringing of a bell at 9:30 a.m. President Ronald Reagan made this famous during his reelection campaign in 1985.

11. The most expensive stock in the world is Berkshire Hathaway. The company owns Dairy Queen, Geico, and Duracell. They also own huge stakes in Coca-Cola and American Express. The company's stock is $320,250 per share (October 2020) since the company never did a stock split, meaning that it never devalued the worth of a single share.

12. The Amsterdam Stock Exchange was the world's first. It was established in 1602.

13. Australia has had the best performing share market in the world from 1900 to 2009.

14. Women first worked on the New York Stock Exchange in 1943 due to a shortage of male workers during World War 2. For the first half of the twentieth century, the New York Stock Exchange was open exclusively to men. From 1943 to 1947, women worked on the stock exchange floor. Women were banned again until 1965 until Muriel "Mickie" Siebert bought a seat on the exchange. She was the only woman working on the exchange for ten years,

earning her the name, "First Lady of Wall Street." A room on the seventh floor is named in her honor.

Facts about people

- People are greedy.
- People are dependable.
- People are mean.
- People are kind.
- People are unpredictable.
- People have routines.
- People love.
- People hate.
- People are mentally unstable.
- People are resilient.
- People are lazy.
- People are innovative.
- People ae pessimistic.
- People help change the world.

As you can see, the stock market works off commodities, assets, and global economies. Humans work off an entirely different set of variables. Human beings can be your greatest investment because the upside of that investment is limitless; however, when they don't pan out, be prepared for a worse outcome than the Great Depression.

The worst kind of people

RAT and RATS (resentful, angry, and treacherous and resentful, angry, and treacherous scoundrels). There are an estimated seven billion rats in the world. That's almost one rat for every human. They carry infectious diseases and cause millions of dollars in damage to infrastructures throughout the world each year. Those are the animal version that nature and God created. These creatures cannot control what they are because they have no mental capacity to change the way they live and survive; this is what nature intended.

Regarding human beings, this is an entirely different scenario. The acronym used in the beginning of this section describes the human version I consider a human rat to be. There are also millions of this species of human running around the planet, causing all kinds of mischief and misery. As my brother and instructor, Soke Ray Rivera, would say, "We have to take out the garbage when its necessary." By no means do I enjoy nor do I even like to look at my fellow man, woman, and child like a disease-infested rodent, but sometimes the shoe just fits. Resentful, angry, and treacherous people sometimes don't even know or even have the mental and spiritual ability to even understand why they are the way they exist. That's why people with a higher sense of being and intellect need to remain above these petty types of people and soar high in the clouds like the eagles do.

SHEEP (systematically helping everyone else progress). Now, let's get to the next type of people to avoid. The sheep of the world continue to drive humankind into the abyss with their goofy-minded actions. Social media and the internet in one perspective can boost one's ego, business, reunite old friends and family, help break criminal cases for the greater good, etc. On the other hand, social media and the internet and countless other life factors and platforms continue to allow the SHEEP to dictate how other people progress through life. Where are the leaders, the innovators, the social activists with the character to stand up and say, "Hey, I'm not for the buffoonery or the monkey business"? P. T. Barnum, the founder of the Ringling Brothers and Barnum and Bailey circus, famously said, "There's a sucker born every day." In this twenty-first century of the Gen Z and millennial-based society, there are too many suckers. TikTok, Instagram thirst traps, YouTube, and TMZ lead videos and interviews got the life game really messed up for the culture of new potential leaders for our future here in America and around the world. Tigers don't lose sleep over the opinion of sheep; unfortunately, there aren't too many tigers left.

> We are all born ignorant, but one must
> work hard to remain stupid. (Benjamin Franklin)

If you're older than five years old, you know right from wrong. (Khoury R. Porter)

A lie gets halfway around the world until the truth gets its boots on and then eventually chases it down. (Mark Twain)

True power rest behind the throne. (Anonymous)

What I did yesterday will not work in the present and what I do in the present will not work tomorrow. (Khoury R. Porter)

Chapter 6

What We Think We Know, Learned, and Believe

Religion, the big three, and more

Religion—a personal set or institutionalized system of religious attitudes, beliefs, and practices.

Judaism

- Judaism is the world's oldest monotheistic religion, dating back nearly four thousand years.
- Abraham is credited with being the founder of the faith.
- More than one thousand years after Abraham, the prophet Moses led the Israelites out of Egypt.
- Traditionally, a person is considered Jewish if his or her mother is Jewish.
- Six types of Judaism: (1) Orthodox, (2) Ultraorthodox, (3) Reform, (4) Conservative, (5) Reconstructionist, and (6) Humanistic.

Christianity

- An Abrahamic monotheistic religion based on the life and teachings of Jesus of Nazareth.
- The world's largest religion, with 2.8 billion followers.

- Christianity began as a second temple Judaic sect in the first-century Hellenistic Judaism in the Roman province of Judea.
- Christianity has many sects/divisions: (1) Catholic, (2) Greek Orthodox, (3) Oriental Orthodox, (4) Protestant: Baptist, Mormon, etc.

Islam

- Founded by the prophet Mohammed in AD 613.
- Two forms of Islam: Sunni and Shiites.
- Islam means "submission" to the will of God.
- The second largest religion in the world, with 1.8 billion followers.
- Muslims are monotheistic and worship one all-knowing God, who in Arabic is known as Allah.

Buddhism

- Founded in India 563–483 BCE by Siddhartha Gautama, aka Buddha.
- Buddhists believe that human life is a cycle of suffering and rebirth but that if one achieves a state of enlightenment, it is possible to escape this cycle forever.
- Buddhists do not believe in any kind of deity or god; although there are supernatural figures who can help or hinder people on the path toward enlightenment.
- Buddhists believe in reincarnation.
- There are two main groups in Buddhism: Mahayana Buddhism and Theravada Buddhism.

School, education, and real life

Twenty life skills not taught in school

- Conversation skills
- How to think
- How to manage money
- Dating and romance
- Your legal rights
- How to live minus technology
- Home repair and insurance
- Car repair and insurance
- Credit score and credit cards
- Cooking
- Religion and spirituality
- Manners
- Gun safety
- How to find and get a job
- Health care and health insurance
- Self defense
- Learning from failure
- Time management
- Government and the law

What we learn in school (kindergarten to fifth grade)

Kindergarten

- Being in a routine
- Learn to follow rules
- The fundamentals of learning
- Basic math, basic reading and writing, and science

First grade

- Learn how to identify and create a story's beginning, middle, and end
- The basics of writing
- Learn earth, life, and physical sciences
- Entry-level social studies, ex.: cities, towns, states, nations, etc.

Second grade

- Form friendships, patience, increased concentration, and self-control
- Learn how to tell time and count money
- Independent reading is encouraged
- Entry-level computer skills

Third grade

- Learn fractions, multiplication, and how to measure weight and volume
- Learn how to find information in books
- Learn how to write essays
- Learn global places and more intricate science

Fourth grade

- Learn organization and time management
- Socialization skills become more of a priority
- Competitiveness among your peers starts
- Advance skills in math, reading, writing, science, social studies, technology

Fifth grade

- Learn to put all the academic pieces together
- Students are expected to take more responsibility

Middle school, aka junior high school

- Make good friend choices
- Work in teams and negotiate conflict
- Manage a student-teacher mismatch
- Create organization and homework systems
- Monitor and take responsibility for grades
- Learn to self-advocate
- Self-regulate emotions
- Cultivate passions and recognize limitations
- Make responsible, safe, and ethical choices
- Create and innovate

High school

- Figure out your strengths and interests
- Develop problem solving, analytical skills, and critical thinking
- Learn how to network for future career opportunities
- Find mentor(s) and mentorship opportunities

Colleges and universities

- Offer second and four-year degrees only
- Smaller than universities when it comes to student enrollment
- Include community, liberal arts, career colleges; technical, trade, and vocational schools are also colleges

University

- Offer four-year master and doctorate degrees
- Tend to be in the larger scale in terms of enrollment

College and university stats and facts

- Four in ten Americans aged twenty-five and older have a bachelor's degree.
- Women are more likely to graduate from college than men.
- Asian Americans have the most college degree representation at 61 percent, followed by white adults at 42 percent, 28 percent of Black adults, and 21 percent of Hispanic adults.
- 62 percent of students who start a degree or certificate finish within six years.
- Business is the most held four-year degree, followed by health care.
- Adults aged twenty-two to twenty-nine with a four-year degree earn $52,000, compared to full-time workers with a high school diploma at $30,000 a year.
- The unemployment rate is lower for college graduates than workers without a four-year degree.
- Recent college graduates are more likely than graduates to be underemployed. This means they are working in jobs that do not require college degrees.
- When it comes to income and wealth accumulation, first-generation college graduates lag substantially behind those with college-educated parents.
- Most Americans see value in their degrees.

What exactly have we learned? What do we actually know, and do we believe?

So, as we just learned from all the information we just read, we have taken in a lot from the faiths we were given and the school systems we all were brought up in. The religious beliefs of the big three have given millions direction on a spiritual and moral level. School gave us numerous basic life skills that we are supposed to utilize and achieve life success with them. However, do we believe wholeheartedly in what our teachers, priests, pastors, imam, or professors have told us? Religion gives depth to those people who cannot find peace and spiritual enlightenment out in the world. School at any level gives us the basic and advance knowledge to go out into the wilderness of the world and try to make something good out of nothing. Many a man has used the vessels and platforms of religion and the diplomas and certifications from the schools they have attended to obtain their goals and have an impact on the world. At the end of the day, if you don't honestly believe in yourself, the religious faith and the degree you obtain are worth nothing at all.

Chapter 7

Does School Really Make Me Money?

In today's twenty-first century, we have seen that formal education for some doesn't really matter in the aspect of making money at a decent wage that a person can live a decently comfortable life. However, not everyone will luck up with being a Fashion Nova model and spokesperson, or a YouTube sensation with a channel with a million followers and thousands, if not millions, of views of their videos, which causes advertisers to cut you a check. Most people in life will have to resort to working for someone else to make a living and take care of themselves and their family. Let's look at some of the numbers and see if school and a degree from college and/or a university helps the common non-Instagram-famous influencer.

How does a college degree improve a graduate's earning and employment?

- Bachelor's degree holders will make $1 million more in lifetime earnings than high school diploma earners.
- Annual median earnings for workers aged twenty-two to twenty-seven is $22,500 for a high school diploma and $43,000 for a bachelor's degree.
- Bachelor's degree holders are 47 percent more likely to have health insurance through their jobs than those with high

school diplomas. Their employees contribute more to their health coverage to the tune of 74 percent.

Lifetime earnings by level of education

- High school diploma—$1,304,000
- Some college—$1,547,000
- Associate degree—$1,727,000
- Bachelor's degree—$2,268,000
- Master's to PhD—$2,671,000

Twenty-five highest-paid occupations in the United States

- Anesthesiologists—$331,190
- Oral and maxillofacial surgeons—$311,460
- Obstetricians and gynecologists—$296,210
- Surgeons—$294,520
- Orthodontists—$267,280
- Physicians—$255,110
- Psychiatrists—$249,760
- Internal medicine physicians—$235,930
- Chief executives—$213,020
- Nurse anesthetists—$202,470
- Pediatricians—$198,420
- Airline pilots and flight engineers—$198,190
- Dentists—$175,160
- Computer and information systems managers—$162,930
- Dentists (general)—$167,160
- Architectural and engineering managers—$158,970
- Natural sciences managers—$156,110
- Financial managers—$153,440
- Physicists—$151,580
- Judges—$148,030
- Podiatrists—$145,840
- Petroleum engineers—$145,720
- Prosthodontists—$143,730

Thirty-two jobs that pay $100k without an advanced degree

1. Commercial pilot
    * Average income—$93,000
    * Entry-level income—$47,570
    * High earning potential—$200,920
2. Web developers and digital interface designers
    * Average income—$77,200
    * Entry-level income—$40,750
    * High earning potential—$146,430
3. Computer programmer
    * Average income—$89,190
    * Entry-level income—$51,440
    * High earning potential—$146,050
4. Animator or multimedia artist
    * Average income—$68,800
    * Entry-level income—$27,860
    * High earning potential—$116,350
5. Detective / criminal investigator
    * Average income—$86,940
    * Entry-level income—$46,020
    * High earning potential—$146,000
6. Writer or editor
    * Average income—$67,730
    * Entry-level income—$36,380
    * High earning potential—$100,000+
7. Sound-engineering technician
    * Average income—$53,520
    * Entry-level income—$27,650
    * High earning income—$119,720
8. Sales representative
    * Average income—$58,770
    * Entry-level income—$29,110
    * High earning income—$128,820

9. Real estate agent
    - Average income—$49,040
    - Entry-level income—$25,100
    - High earning income—$112,410
10. Computer network support specialist
    - Average income—$65,450
    - Entry-level income—$40,620
    - High earning income—$110,450

All these careers require one year of training.

Jobs paying over $100k with only two to four-year degrees

11. Computer and information systems manager
    - Average income—$151,150
12. Marketing manager
    - Average income—$142,170
13. Sales manager
    - Average income—$132,290
14. Human resources manager
    - Average income—$121,220
15. Purchasing manager
    - Average income—$125,940
    - High income—$197,630
16. Air traffic controller
    - Average income—$130,420
    - High income—$184,780
17. Medical or health services manager
    - Average income—$104,280
    - High income—$195,630
18. Art director
    - Average income—$97,270
    - High income—$199,250
19. Computer network architect
    - Average income—$116,780
    - High income—$175,570

20. Film or video editor
    - Average income—$67,250
    - High income—$152,720
21. Administrative services and facilities managers
    - Average income—$98,890
    - High income—$169,930
22. Construction manager
    - Average income—$97,180
    - High income—$169,070
23. Software developer
    - Average income—$105,310
    - High income—$167,460
24. Funeral home manager
    - Average income—$74,200
    - High income—$156,940
25. Information security analyst
    - Average income—$103,590
    - High income—$163,300
26. Fashion designer
    - Average income—$75,810
    - High income—$146,300
27. Network administrator
    - Average income—$84,810
    - High income—$134,970
28. Property manager
    - Average income—$59,660
    - High income—$134,570
29. Accountant
    - Average income—$65,810
    - High income—$127,410
30. Market research analyst
    - Average income—$65,810
    - High income—$127,410
31. Public relations specialist
    - Average income—$62,810
    - High income—$118,210

32. Social or community services manager
    - Average income—$69,600
    - High income—$115,800

Everyone will not become a TikTok viral sensation, an Instagram influencer, a hugely successful YouTuber, a rapper, a model, an actor, or something else in life that is off the regular path to success. Someone must fly planes, someone must perform surgeries, and someone must fix busted pipes. School in any form will give you a guarantee to success. School or formal training might not be for everyone; however, never give up on education no matter what form it comes in. Education does not have to happen behind a desk in a stuffy lecture room. It will come from all aspects of life. Remember to always embrace knowledge and accept its gifts.

> All hard work brings a profit but mere talk
> leads only to poverty. (Proverbs 14:23)

> Life is like a fruit tree. At the top of the tree,
> you can pick fruit from your labor, but the roots
> of your foundation lie deep beneath the surface.
> (Khoury R. Porter)

> You can't prepare for life with a C+ perfor-
> mance and expect A+ results. (Khoury R. Porter)

Chapter 8

Land of the Free, or Is It?

Laws to live by

Criminal offenses and conditions in the United States:

- Felonies
- Misdemeanors
- Violations
- Criminal charge
- Probation
- Parole

Felony—a crime typically, one involving violence; regarded as more serious than a misdemeanor, and usually punishable by imprisonment for more than one year or by death.

Misdemeanor—a crime punishable by less than one year in jail.

Violations—failure or refusal to follow any applicable state or federal law, such that criminal and/or civil penalties may be imposed.

Criminal charge—a formal accusation made by a governmental authority, asserting that somebody has committed a crime.

Probation—a period of supervision over an offender, ordered by the court in lieu of incarceration.

Types of felonies

- Robbery
- Arson
- Kidnapping
- Burglary
- Driving under the influence
- Manslaughter
- Assault with or without a weapon
- Grand theft auto
- Rape
- Possession of an unlawful firearm
- Treason
- Sodomy
- Fraud (can be a misdemeanor)
- Murder
- Criminally negligent homicide
- Grand larceny
- Credit-card fraud (can be misdemeanor)
- Forgery
- Strangulation
- Vehicular assault

Types of misdemeanors

- Disorderly conduct
- DUI
- Reckless driving
- Mischief
- Vandalism
- Indecent exposure
- Theft
- Trespass
- Petit larceny
- Perjury
- Shoplifting
- Menacing
- Harassment

Felony classes and sentence guidelines in New York State:

Class A felony
- fifteen to twenty-five years
- Possibility of life

Class nonviolent felony
- Non-predicate felon—five to twenty-five years
- Predicate felon—eight to twenty-five years
- Violent predicate felon—ten to twenty-five years

Class B nonviolent felony
- Non-predicate felon—1 to 3 years up to 8 1/3 to 25 years
- Predicate felon—4 1/2 to 9 years up to 12 1/2 to 25 years

Class C violent felony
- Non-predicate ranges from no incarceration up to 3 1/2 to 15 years
- Predicate felon—five to fifteen years
- Violent predicate felon—seven to fifteen years

Class C nonviolent felony
- Non-predicate felon ranges from no incarceration up to five to fifteen years
- Predicate felon—3 to 6 years up to 7 1/2 to 15 years

Class D violent felony
- Non-predicate felon—two to seven years
- Predicate felon—three to seven years
- Violent predicate felon—five to seven years

Class D nonviolent felony
- Non-predicate felon ranges from no incarceration up to 2 1/3 to 7 years
- Predicate felon 2 to 4 years up to 3 1/2 to 7 years

Class E violent felony
- Non-predicate felon—1 1/2 to 4 years
- Predicate felon—two to four years
- Violent predicate felon—three to four years

Class E nonviolent felony

- Non-predicate felon ranges from no incarceration up to 1 1/3 to 4 years
- Predicate felon—1 1/2 to 3 years up to a maximum of 2 to 4 years

Misdemeanor classes and sentence guidelines in NYS:

- *Class A.* Community service, a fine, mandatory state surcharges, order of protections, probation, and one year in county jail.
- *Class B.* Fines, state surcharges, community service, order of protection, probation, and jail time up to ninety days.
- *Unclassified.* Found in the vehicle and traffic law and NYS Penal Law.
- *Violations.* Fines, mandatory state surcharge, community service, order of protection, or up to fifteen days in jail.

Miranda rights

1. You have the *right* to remain *silent.*
2. *Anything you say* can be *used against you* in a court of law.
3. You have the *right* to have an attorney present.
4. If you cannot afford an attorney, one will be appointed to you.

Never speak to any law enforcement agency, officer, district attorney, state attorney general, or federal prosecutor without speaking with your attorney. Then, with your attorney's advice, then can you speak to those people mentioned above.

> Have many friends and treat them well,
> but never your secrets tell. Because the day your
> friend becomes your foe, out into the world all
> your secrets go. (Marion Green, mom)

The Bill of Rights of the United States

1. Freedom of religion, speech, press, assembly, and petition
2. Right to keep and bear arms in order to maintain a well-regulated militia
3. No quartering of soldiers
4. Freedom from unreasonable searches and seizures
5. Right to due process of law, freedom from self-incrimination, and double jeopardy
6. Rights of accused persons to have a speedy and public trial
7. Right of trial by jury in civil cases
8. Freedom from excessive bail, cruel and unusual punishments
9. Other rights
10. Rights reserved to the states or the people
11. Lawsuits against states
12. Presidential elections
13. Abolition of slavery
14. Civil rights
15. Black suffrage
16. Income taxes
17. Senatorial elections
18. Prohibition of alcohol
19. Women's suffrage
20. Terms of office
21. Repeal of prohibition
22. Term limits for the presidency
23. Washington, D. C., suffrage
24. Abolition of poll taxes
25. Presidential succession
26. Eighteen-year-old suffrage
27. Congressional pay raises

Supreme Court cases that changed America

Brown v. Board of Education (1954). Separate schools are not equal.

Cooper v. Aaron (1958). States cannot nullify decisions of the federal courts.

Gideon v. Wainwright (1963). Indigent defendants must be provided representation without charge.

Mapp v. Ohio (1961). Illegally obtained material cannot be used in a criminal trial.

Miranda v. Arizona (1966). Police must inform suspects of their rights before questioning.

Terry v. Ohio (1968). Stop and frisks do not violate the Constitution under certain circumstances.

Texas v. Jonson (1989). Even offensive speech, such as flag burning, is protected by the First Amendment.

Roe v. Wade (1973). A woman has a right to choose to have a baby, not be regulated by state or federal, and not to have an abortion.

I spent seven years as a Westchester County corrections officer in Valhalla, New York. I have personally interacted and was responsible for the care, custody, and control of thousands of people from many different ethnicities, education levels, religious beliefs, cultures, and gender identifications. Westchester county in the start of 2009 started to accept and house federal inmates due to numerous federal contracts the department acquired with various federal law enforcement agencies. So I had the ability to learn about federal cases in conjunction with learning about local and state-level criminal cases. I learned a lot about the criminal justice system in those years spent at the Norwood E. Jackson Correctional Facility, aka Valhalla. What I can say about the judicial system on a hold is that it is not a place for rehabilitation. It is a place for punishment and for the encouragement for recidivism of its inmate inhabitants. The power of choice is one option you have in this world to help keep you from behind bars. The power of choice, as powerful as it may be, is not the only thing with the power to keep you out of jail or prison. The power of the male figure or a father is just as powerful. In the next chapter, we will dive into the power of a dad.

Chapter 9

The Power of a Father

Thirty-six shocking statistics on fatherless homes

In the United States, as of 2018, 64 million men identified themselves as fathers; 26.5 million men out of the 64 million were married to a spouse and having children under the age of eighteen. According to the US Census Bureau, 22 percent of fathers at this time were raising three or more children under the age of eighteen. The following information is from 2018.

1. 85 percent of youth who are currently in prison grew up in a fatherless home (Texas Department of Corrections).
2. Seven out of every ten youth that are housed in state-operated correctional facilities, including detention and residential treatment, come from a fatherless home (US Department of Justice).
3. 39 percent of students in the United States, from the first grade to their senior year of high school, do not have a father at home. Children without a fathers are four times more likely to be living in poverty than children with a father (National Public Radio).
4. Children from fatherless homes are twice as likely to drop out from school before graduating than children who have fathers in their lives (National Public Radio).
5. 24.7 million children in the United States live in a home where their biological father is not present. That equates to

one in every three children in the United States not having access to their father (National Public Radio).

6. Girls who live in a fatherless home have a 100 percent higher risk of suffering from obesity than girls who have their father present. Teen girls from fatherless homes are also four times more likely to become mothers before the age of twenty (National Public Radio).

7. 57 percent of the fatherless homes in the United States involve African American / Black households. Hispanic households have a 31 percent fatherless rate, while Caucasian/White households have a 20 percent fatherless rate (National Public Radio).

8. In 2011, 44 percent of children in homes headed by a single mother were living in poverty. Just 12 percent of children in married-couple families were living in poverty (US Census Bureau).

9. Children who live in a single-parent home are more than two times more likely to commit suicide than children in two-parent home (*Lancet*).

10. 72 percent of Americans believe that a fatherless home is the most significant social and family problem that is facing their country (National Center for Fathering).

11. Only 68 percent of children will spend their entire childhood with an intact family (US Census Bureau).

12. 75 percent of rapists are motivated by displaced anger that is associated with feelings of abandonment that involves their father (US Department of Justice).

13. Living in a fatherless home is a contributing factor to substance abuse, with children from such homes accounting for 75 percent of adolescent patients being treated in substance abuse centers (US Department of Justice).

14. 85 percent of all children which exhibit some type of a behavioral disorder come from a fatherless home (US Department of Justice).

15. 90 percent of the youth in the United States who decide to run away from home, or become homeless for any reason,

originally come from a fatherless home (US Department of Justice).

16. 63 percent of youth suicides involve a child who was living a fatherless home when they made their final decision (US Department of Justice).
17. Children who live in a single parent or stepfamily home report less schoolwork monitoring, less social supervision, and lower educational expectations than children who came from two-parent homes (*American Sociological Review*).
18. Even when poverty levels are equal, children who come from two-parent home outperform children who come from a one parent home (US Department of Health and Human Services).
19. Within the African American / Black community, about 2.5 million fathers live with their children while 1.7 million fathers are not living with them (Huffington Post).
20. In a 2014 study, only 3 percent of single mothers fell into the strongest demographic groups while 44 percent fell into the weakest demographic groups (Brookings).
21. About 40 percent of children in the United States are born to mothers who are not married. Over 60 percent of these children were born to mothers who were under the age thirty.
22. 25 percent of children aged eighteen are currently being raised without the presence of a father. Around 50 percent of single mothers have never married; 29 percent are divorced. Only one in five are either separated or widowed.
23. In single-mother households, 50 percent involve just one child; 30 percent of single mothers are raising two children on their own (US Census Bureau).
24. 27 percent of single mothers were jobless for the entire year while taking care of their children. Only 22 percent of those who were out of work were receiving unemployment benefits at the time (US Census Bureau).
25. The median income for a household with a single mother is $35,400. The median income for a home with a mar-

ried couple raising their children is $85,300 in the United States. Two-thirds of low-income working families with children are in the African American community (US Census Bureau).

26. Over 30 percent of fatherless homes are classified as being food insecure, yet only 13 percent of homes will utilize the services of a food pantry. Over 30 percent of fatherless homes also spend more than half of their income on housing costs, which classifies the household as experiencing a severe housing burden (US Department of Agriculture).

27. In the United States, Mississippi has the highest number of fatherless homes, with 36 percent of households falling into the category. Louisiana comes in second at 34 percent while Alabama is third at 31 percent (US Census Bureau).

28. Children who live in a fatherless home are 279 percent more likely to deal drugs or carry firearms for offensive purposes compared to children who live their fathers (Allen and Lo).

29. 92 percent of the parents who are currently in prison in the United States are fathers (Glaze and Maruschak).

30. Pregnant women who do not have the support of the father experience pregnancy loss at a 48 percent rate. When the father is present, the prevalence of pregnancy loss falls to 22 percent.

31. For single dads, 39 percent of households had a family income which was $50,000 or more; 44 percent of single dads were divorced while only 33 percent had never married (US Census Bureau).

32. 43 percent of fathers do not see their role as something that is important to their personal identity; 54 percent of fathers in the United States say that parenting isn't enjoyable all the time (Pew Research).

33. Even in homes with fathers, the modern dad spends only eight hours per week on childcare, which is six hours less than modern mom. On the other hand, 43 percent of the modern dad's time is spent with paid work, compared to

25 percent of the time for the modern mom. Dads are spending three times more time with their kids than dads did in 1965 (Pew Research).

34. Only 5 percent of households in the United States say that the ideal situation is to have the mother work and the father stay home to take care of the children (Pew Research).

35. 53 percent of Americans say that mothers do a better job at parenting than fathers. Only 1 percent of Americans say that fathers can do a better job at parenting than mothers (Pew Research).

36. 70 percent of adults say it is equally important for a newborn to spend time bonding with their father and their mother (Pew Research).

Jay-Z once said, "Men and women lie, numbers don't." Statistics and facts don't have the ability to fabricate the situation if taken from valid sources of information. Another famous quote is, "The truth hurts." If all this data is correct, then we in the male community need to really step up and do a better job for ourselves, our families, and our communities. Culturally speaking, it pains me to know that men in the Black community have the highest rates of separation from our families. Mass incarceration was and still is the leading cause of this problem, including violent death by firearm. For my Caucasian boys and men, your problems are the same in some of your communities. If you are the product of the trailer park, the ultra-rural Southern and Midwestern communities of the United States, or the product of alcoholism or crystal meth–addicted parents, then you to have been a victim of this phenomena.

On the other side of the spectrum, we have fathers and men of college educated and corporate-based backgrounds who, on paper, look and play the part of the so-called great father. The police officer and firefighter, blue-collar American man who once served our country in the armed forces is praised by all as the ideal father for our sons. A corporate CEO and hedge-fund manager gets looked at with awe that he has some divine halo because he makes high six or seven figures. Little Puppet from East Los Angeles to Chief Rainwater from the Navajo Nation, who lives on a reservation, all deserve the same respect as a man and a father. Every man and especially every father has a duty to rise to the occasion to break the cycle of evil men and smash the numbers of statistics into the netherworld. I took an unspoken oath when I made my son and decided to raise my stepson that as their father, I would never leave them stranded on the battle-field of life. Each man should do the same.

Chapter 10

Mind, Body, and Soul

No person can achieve true balance in their life without having all three of life's pillars in total unison. The mind, body, and soul must be always healthy to keep balance and be at true peace. Let's look how we can achieve this balance by breaking down and understanding these pillars.

The three pillars of health

1. Mental
2. Physical
3. Spiritual/emotional/soul

Mental health

The human brain is three pounds of remarkable organic matter. Keeping your brain healthy is an intricate and vital part of your life. Illness of the mind show up in different versions of imbalance. Here is a list to recognize some of these disorders in yourself or in the people around you.

Anxiety disorders is a group of mental health disorders that includes social phobias, agoraphobia, post-traumatic stress disorder.

Behavioral and emotional disorders (usually in children)

- Oppositional defiant disorder
- Conduct disorder
- Attention deficit hyperactivity disorder

Bipolar affective disorder, formerly known as manic depression. People experience episodes of mania (elation) and depression. The exact cause is unknown, but a genetic predisposition has been clearly established. Environmental stressors can also trigger episodes of this mental illness.

Depression is a mood disorder characterized by lowering of mood, loss of interest and enjoyment, and reduced energy. Symptoms of depression can lead to increased risk of suicidal thoughts or behaviors.

Dissociation and dissociative disorders. Dissociation is a mental process where a person disconnects from their thoughts, feelings, memories, or sense of identity.

Different types

- Dissociative amnesia
- Dissociative fugue
- Depersonalization disorder
- Dissociative identity disorder

Eating disorders

- Anorexia nervosa—restricted eating
- Bulimia nervosa—periods of binge-eating, followed by attempts to compensate with excessive exercise, vomiting, or periods of strict dieting
- Binge eating

Obsessive-compulsive disorder

- OCD is an anxiety disorder.
- Obsessions—recurrent thoughts, images, or impulses that are intrusive and unwanted.
- Compulsions—time-consuming and distressing repetitive rituals.

Paranoia is the irrational and persistent feeling that people are out to get you. Paranoia may be a symptom of conditions, including paranoid personality disorder, delusional (paranoid) disorder, and schizophrenia.

Post-traumatic stress disorder (PTSD) is a mental health condition that can develop as a response to any traumatic event. Car crashes, physical or sexual assault, war-related events, torture, or natural disasters can cause PTSD.

Psychosis

- Delusions
- Hallucinations
- Confused thinking
- It can occur in a number of mental illnesses.
- Medication and psychological support can relieve, or even eliminate, psychotic symptoms.

Schizophrenia is characterized by disruptions to thinking and emotions and a distorted perception of reality. Symptoms vary widely but may include hallucinations, delusions, thought disorder, social withdrawal, lack of motivation, and impaired thinking and memory. People with schizophrenia have a high risk of suicide.

Physical health

Physical health can be broken into two parts. Your physique and your nutritional health make up the physical department of your health. Exercises such as jumping jacks, push-ups, and mountain climbers tone your muscles, while weightlifting makes your muscle groups stronger and denser. Running, jogging, and bike-riding strengthen your cardiovascular system. A well-balanced diet—whether you are a vegan down to a traditional omnivore—will make sure your organs, connective tissues, and cells function properly.

Spiritual/emotional health (soul)

Spiritual health is having the ability to connect with the universe and/or with the higher power called *God*. Atheists have the right not to believe in God or a higher power concept. In my lifetime, I have seen and have been a recipient of what I believe to be divine, spiritual, or downright from God himself, special blessings, and protections. Can I explain or prove for a 100 percent fact to a nonspiritual or non-God-believing person of my experiences? No, I cannot. This is the same way that a nonbeliever in the divine order of things cannot prove me wrong for believing in God. Having some sort of spiritual balance is essential to all humankind. Since the beginning of humanity, people have believed in the divine doctrines of the universe to help them explain life's mysteries. Emotional balance is the core of human self. How can you call yourself a human being and not feel love, hate, resentment, embarrassment, or hope? Hormones, endorphins, dopamine, and a host of other chemicals in the body and brain help us feel or not feel in a healthy or unhealthy way.

Total balance of mind, physical, and spiritual/emotional health must be always kept in balance so that you keep healthy and fully charged of positive energy. When these three phases are out of sorts, life progression stops, and stagnation will continue to be your reality. Men, boys, and males in general don't keep their three pillars in balance and properly nourished.

Information to keep you mentally and physically fit

The human body and our health

- The longest cells in the human body are the motor neurons. They can be up to four and half feet long and run from the lower spinal cord to the big toe.
- The longest living cells in the body are brain cells.
- The brain requires more than 25 percent of the oxygen that is used by the human body.
- Fifteen million blood cells are produced and destroyed in the human body every second.

Twelve activities to burn calories and fat

- Running—burns 450 calories every thirty minutes. Helps cardiorespiratory development, leg strength, and endurance.
- Rock climbing—burns 371 calories every thirty minutes. Strength, endurance, and flexibility increases.
- Swimming—burns 360 calories in a half hour. It's an overall body workout.
- Cycling—burns three hundred to four hundred calories every thirty minutes. It's a great cardio workout that builds up thighs and calves.
- Boxing—burns 324–500 calories in thirty minutes. Calories can burn for hours after training. Increases muscle tone, strengthens your bones, and reduces osteoporosis. Improves core stability and improves muscular endurance. Improves coordination and body awareness. It increases reflexes, fine and gross motor skills.
- Racquetball—burns three hundred calories in a thirty-minute session. It builds lower body strength and endurance. It also develops flexibility in your abs and back.

- Basketball—burns three hundred calories in a thirty-minute session. It develops flexibility, endurance, and cardiorespiratory health.
- Rowing—burns about 280 calories per half hour. Endurance, strength, shoulders, thighs, and biceps all get built with this workout.
- Tennis—it burns 250–300 calories in a half-hour session. It develops cardiorespiratory function.
- Cross-country skiing—270 calories burned in a thirty-minute session. Cross-country skiing is great for interval training.
- Ice-skating—gives you all the benefits of running without the joint stress; 252 calories are burned in a thirty-minute session.
- Swing dancing—180 calories burned in a thirty-minute session. Flexibility, core strength, and endurance increases with this activity.

You are what you eat

The difference between fruits and veggies

Botany definition of a fruit and vegetable

- Fruit is the mature, sexually produced, seed-bearing ovary of a flowering plant.
- Vegetable comes from the vegetative or nonsexual parts of the plant (leaves, roots, stems).

Culinary definition of a fruit

- Fruit—the edible, fleshy part of a perennial plant associated with its flower, which tastes good due to its astringency, acid content, and sugars.

The difference between herbs and spices

- Herbs are the aromatic leaves of plants, and they come from temperate regions of the world.
- Spices consist of the seeds, buds, fruit or flower parts, and bark or roots of aromatic and pungent plants, usually from tropical regions.

Popeye was one of my favorite childhood cartoons. Let's look at why he could beat Bluto every time after eating spinach. Spinach contains 14,580 units of vitamin A. It has 583 milligrams of potassium and 167 grams of calcium.

Seventy percent of the human body is water, as well as our planet. I need for you to understand the importance of H_2O.

Different types of drinking water

- *Still water* is water without bubbles, including tap water, drinking water sold in large containers, and mineral.
- *Sparkling nature water* is tap water or underground water that contains carbon dioxide gas, either manufactured or naturally occurring in the ground.
- *Seltzer* is common tap water that has been filtered and carbonated.
- *Mineral water* is any water containing dissolved minerals, whether from an underground or surface water source. Natural mineral water, usually spring water, contains whatever minerals were in it when it came out of the ground.
- *Club soda* is carbonated water that has had mineral salts such as bicarbonates, citrates, and phosphates of sodium added.

Vitamins: "The big thirteen"

- *Vitamin A* is essential growth and cell development, healthy skin, hair, bones, and teeth. It's found in salmon and other cold-water fish, egg yolks, and fortified dairy products.
- *Vitamin C* supports immunity, promotes wound healing, helps your body absorb iron, and it acts as a key antioxidant. It's found in citrus fruits, melons, berries, peppers, broccoli, and potatoes.
- *Vitamin D* aids in the absorption of calcium and helps keep your bones strong (sunlight, fortified milk, butter, egg yolk, fish, and fish-liver oil).
- *Vitamin E* is an important antioxidant that helps maintain muscles and red blood cells. It is found in eggs, vegetable oils, nuts, seeds, and fortified cereals.
- *Vitamin K* is essential for proper blood-clotting (spinach, green leafy vegetables, and liver).
- *Thiamine (Vitamin B1)* plays an important role in regulating your metabolism. Thiamine also helps maintain proper nerve function and normal digestion. Pork, legumes, nuts, seeds, grains, and fortified cereals will help you meet your body's vitamin B1 needs.
- *Riboflavin (Vitamin B2)* supports normal vision and healthy skin, aids in adrenal function and contributes to a healthy metabolism (lean meat, poultry, dairy products, raw mushrooms, grains, fortified cereals, and soy/rice beverages).
- *Niacin (Vitamin B3)* promotes normal growth, helps lower cholesterol levels, and supports your metabolism. Lean meats, poultry, seafood, milk, eggs, legumes, fortified bread, and cereals to get your vitamin B3.
- *Pantothenic acid (Vitamin B5)* normalizes blood sugar levels and synthesizes cholesterol, hemoglobin, and hormones. All (almost) foods provide it.
- *Pyridoxine (Vitamin B6)* promotes the metabolism of both proteins and carbohydrates, helping your body to release energy. It also supports proper nerve function. Meat, fish,

poultry, bananas, green leafy vegetables, potatoes, grains, cereals, and soybeans.

- *Biotin (Vitamin B7)* is essential to regulating your metabolism and can be found in egg yolks, soybeans, whole grains, nuts, and yeast.
- *Folate, Folic Acid (Vitamin B9)* is essential for pregnant women as it helps prevent birth defects. It's necessary to the production of DNA, RNA, and red blood cells. Liver, yeast, leafy green veggies, asparagus, orange juice, avocados, legumes, and fortified flour have folic acid.
- *Cobalamin (Vitamin B12)* helps your body to produce healthy red blood cells, RNA, DNA, and myelin (a component in nerve fibers). Found in all animal products.

Understand your mind

How people learn

- *Visual (spatial learner)*—uses images, pictures, spatial understanding, and sense of sight. These learners are picture smart.
- *Auditory (musical learner)*—uses sound and/or music and sense of hearing. These learners are sound smart.
- *Verbal (linguistic learner)*—prefers words both in speech and writing. These learners are word smart.
- *Logical (mathematical learner)*—focuses on logic reasoning and systems. These learners are math smart.
- *Kinesthetic (physical learner)*—utilizes the body, hands, and sense of touch. These are body smart.
- *Social (interpersonal learner)*—learns in groups or with people. These learners are people smart.
- *Solitary (interpersonal learner)*—works alone and uses self-study. Self-smart people.

Understanding how you learn and how you comprehend the information you just obtained is crucial to the foundation of your success. Growing up in the late 1970s and into the '80s, it was never taught, discussed, or even mentioned in any capacity how your mind learned. Not knowing this deeply increases your chances at failing in life. There are seven different ways to learn, but there are a million and one ways to choose your path to your own unique success.

Chapter 11

Knowledge Is Power

According to Einstein

- "We all know that light travels faster than sound. That's why certain people appear bright until you hear them speak."
- "Wisdom is not a product of schooling but of the lifelong attempt to acquire it."
- "You can never solve a problem on the level on which it was created."
- "A man should look for what is, and not for what he thinks should be."
- "If you can't explain it to a six-year-old, you don't understand it yourself."
- "Two things are infinite: the universe and human stupidity and I'm not sure about the universe."
- "A clever person solves a problem. A wise person avoids it."

Words of Malcolm

- "A man who stands for nothing will fall for anything."
- "Any time you beg and another man to set you free, you will never be free. Freedom is something that you have to do yourselves."
- "If you have no critics, you'll likely have no success."

- "If you have a dog, I must have a dog. If you have a rifle, I must have a rifle. If you have a club, I must have a club. This is equality."
- "Sometimes you have to pick the gun up to put the gun down."
- "I have more respect for a man who lets me know where he stands, even if he's wrong, than the one who comes up like an angel and is nothing but a devil."
- "A wise man can play the part of a clown, but a clown can't play the part of a wise man."

What do I need to start my own business?

- A solid idea
- A product or service
- A business plan
- Three years' savings of your current bills
- 650+ credit score
- A decisive marketing plan for Google and social media
- Proper company structure: LLC, corporation, sole proprietorship

What do I need to buy a home?

- 675 or better credit score
- At least a 5 percent or more down payment of the home sale price
- $10,000 minimum for the closing cost
- One year of property taxes
- Two years' proof of consistent income via your tax returns

The golden era savings plan

Saving money for a rainy day is something you learn from your parents and life experiences. Saving money makes sure that when financial hardships or opportunities come about you are ready to manage them head on. Here are some savings options to help you when you get to fifty-five years old. Some of the following are for the people who work a traditional job.

Types of retirement plans

IRAs (individual retirement arrangements)

- *Traditional IRA*—a tax-advantaged personal savings plan where contributions may be tax deductible.
- *Payroll deduction IRA*—plan is set up by an employer. Employees make contributions by payroll deduction to an IRA they establish with a financial.
- *SEP*—a simplified employee pension plan set up by an employer. Contributions are made by the employer directly to an IRA set up for each employee.
- *Simple IRA*—a savings incentive match plan for employees set up by an employer. Under a simple IRA plan, employees may choose to make salary reduction contributions, and the employer makes matching or non-elective contributions.
- Salary reduction simplified employee pension plan (SARSEP)—a type of SEP set up by an employee before 1997 that includes a salary reduction arrangement.
- Roth IRAs—a Roth IRA is an IRA that, except as explained below, is subject to the rules that apply to a traditional IRA
    - You cannot deduct contributions to a Roth IRA.
    - If you satisfy the requirements, qualified distributions are tax-free.
    - You can make contributions to your Roth IRA after you reach age 70 1/2.
    - You can leave amounts in your Roth IRA as long as you live.
    - The account annuity must be designated as a Roth IRA when it is up.

401(k) plan

- Traditional 401(k)
- Safe harbor 401(k)
- Simple 401(k)
- IRC 403(b) tax-sheltered annuity plan
- Profit-sharing plan
- Defined benefit plan
- Money purchase plan
- Employee stock ownership plans
- 401(a) governmental plans.
- IRC 457 (b) deferred compensation plan

Getting into the habit of saving 10–25 percent of what you make is good habit to develop. Ten percent of $10 = $1.00, and 25 percent of $10.00 = $2.50. Ten percent of $1,000 = $100, and 25 percent = $250. Saving money at this rate will enable you to have a security blanket during financially cold times.

One life is all we have

Life insurance—why you need it

- Life insurance payouts are tax-free. They are not considered income for tax purposes, and your beneficiaries don't have to report the money on their tax returns.
- Your dependents won't have to worry about living expenses. You should have a policy equal to seven to ten times your annual income. The policy should cover the cost of college and other such expenses.
- Life insurance can cover final expenses.
- You can get coverage for chronic and terminal illness.
- Policies can supplement your retirement savings. Cash value on your policy builds up and can be used to buy a car, make a down payment on a car or a home. You can also use it for your retirement.

Who do you trust?

What is a trust fund? A trust fund is an estate planning tool that is a legal entity that holds property or assets for a person or organization. Trust funds can hold a variety of assets, such as money, real property, stocks, bonds, a business, or a combination of many different types of properties or assets. Three parties are required to establish a trust fund: the grantor, the beneficiary, and the trustee. Trust funds are managed by the trustee who must act for the benefit of the grantor and beneficiary. Trust funds can take many forms and can be established under different stipulations. They offer certain tax benefits as well as financial protections and support for those involved.

- A trust fund is designed to hold and manage assets on someone's behalf, with the help of neutral third party.
- Trust funds include a grantor, beneficiary, and trustee.
- The grantor of a trust fund can set terms for the way assets are to be held, gathered, or distributed.
- The trustee manages the fund's assets and executes its directives while the beneficiary receives the assets or other benefits from the fund.
- Trust funds can be revocable and irrevocable, and there are several variations that exist for specific purposes.
  a) The grantor, who sets it up and populates it with their assets
  b) The beneficiary(s) or the person (people) for whom the assets are managed
  c) The trustee, who is a neutral third party (an individual, a trust bank, or another professional fiduciary charged with managing the assets involved)

Trust funds provide certain benefits and protections for those who create the trust and to their beneficiaries. Examples:

- Some types can keep assets held away from any creditors in the event they decide to pursue the grantor's unpaid debts.

- They avoid the need to go through probate, which is the process of analyzing and distributing assets after someone dies without leaving any instructions behind.
- Some trust funds can reduce the amount of estate and inheritance taxes owed after the grantor dies after which the assets are distributed to the beneficiary(s).

Types of trust:

Asset protection. This fund protects a person's assets from their creditor's future claims.

Blind. This fund tries to remove any hint of conflict of interest. As such, the trust fund's grantor and beneficiary have no knowledge of the holdings or how they are managed. It does, however, give control to the trustee.

Charitable. A charitable trust fund benefits a particular charity or the public.

Generation-skipping. This one contains tax benefits when the beneficiary is one of the grantor's grandchildren, or anyone at least 37 1.2 years younger than the grantor.

Grantor retained annuity. Establishing this type of fund allows the grantor to transfer any appreciation of assets to any beneficiaries to minimize estate taxes.

Individual retirement account. Trustees control IRA distributions rather than the beneficiaries.

Land. This allows for the management of property, such as land, a home, or another type of real estate.

Marital. This is funded at one spouse's death and is eligible for the unlimited marital deduction.

Spendthrift. Beneficiaries don't have direct access to the named assets, which means they can't sell, spend, or give away the assets without specific stipulations.

Testamentary. This fund leaves assets to a beneficiary with specific instructions following the grantor's passing.

Annuities

An annuity is a series of payments made at equal intervals. An annuity is a contract between you and an insurance company in which you make a lump-sum payment or a series of payments in exchange for regular disbursements, beginning either immediately or at some point in the future. Depending on how you would like this arrangement to be structured, these retirement income payments could be a set amount fixed or have the potential to grow your income (variable). An annuity is the only financial product that can provide you with a guaranteed lifetime income and protect you from outliving your savings.

Types of annuities:

Variable annuities. The value of a variable annuity is based on the performance of underlying portfolio of investments selected by the annuitant (the annuity owner or the issuing insurance company). Variable annuities have the advantage of letting you control your portfolio; you choose the sub-accounts into which these investments are placed. Consider variable annuities for access to financial markets, growth potential through a wide choice of investment options, and legacy protection.

Income annuity. You can receive a "pension like" payout that helps you maintain the lifestyle you've earned. Consider income annuities for immediate income needs, a worry-free stream of guaranteed income with an option for dividends (dividends are not guaranteed), and the flexibility to design a customized income stream.

Deferred annuity. A deferred annuity begins disbursing payments at a future date chosen by the annuity owner. If you prefer not to put your money in the market, these types of annuities provide a steadier, more-predictable growth approach to your savings. Another benefit is that your premiums grow tax free, leading up to the time when you start receiving payouts. Consider deferred annuities for future income needs, a worry-free stream of guaranteed income, and the flexibility to design to design a customized income stream.

All this knowledge comes with maturity and life experience. Getting older and becoming an old head, as my younger generation would say, is one of the best experiences you can have in life. When you get gray hairs and your back and your knees hurt, it's natural to say, "Damn, I'm old as s———." But you're not old. You're aged, a veteran, a survivor, seasoned, and alive. A male mountain gorilla in the jungles of the Congo doesn't achieve silver back status until he lives long enough to earn his silverish-white hair. The male lion of the Serengeti in Africa earns his mane through hard experiences protecting his pride. Wisdom comes from experience, combined with comprehension of the life events you have lived through and survived from.

Chapter 12

Final Lessons

The American dream

Home ownership. Owning a home is the core of the American dream, family, and ideal ideology in this country. Paying property and school taxes, giving out candy during Halloween, and throwing a fourth of July BBQ is the fabric our culture. Home ownership sets the tone for building a man's foundation of having his own space to call for him and his family to grow and flourish. Let's break down how owning a home progress you forward in life.

- *More stable housing costs.* Fixed rates on your loan keeps your mortgage payment stable from year to year.
- *An appreciating investment.* According to the data firm, Black Knight, the twenty-five-year average appreciation rate of homes in the United States is 3.9 percent per year. Example: you buy a home for $200,000 and it increases in value by 3.9 percent annually, your home would be worth about $233,073 after five years.
- *Opportunity to build equity.* Your home equity is the portion of your home that belongs to you, calculated by subtracting your mortgage balance from the home's market value.
- *Two ways to build equity*: make your monthly mortgage payments and track your home's appreciation over time.

- *A source of ready cash.* A benefit of owning a house is that you can tap your equity to help fund home improvements or pay off personal debt.
- *Home equity loan.* A second mortgage, receive a lump sum of money upfront, then pay it back in installments over a number of years. You can borrow 85 percent of your home's equity.
- *Home equity line of credit (HELOC)* provides access to a line of credit. You can borrow from the line of credit anytime during a "draw period." When that period ends, you have a certain amount of time to pay down the balance. You can borrow 75–85 percent of the value of your home, minus your mortgage balance.
- *Reverse mortgage.* You need to be at least sixty-two years old to apply for this type of loan. Once you receive the money, you'll pay off your mortgage balance and then use the remaining funds as you see fit. The loan is repaid when you die, sell the home, or move out. The amount is based on the equity you have in your home.
- *Tax advantages*: (a) mortgage interest deduction, (b) mortgage insurance premiums, (c) property tax deduction, and (d) capital gains.
- *Helps build credit.*
- *Freedom to personalize your home.*

What makes a person matter in American society according to "them"

- Owning a home
- Having a four-year college degree
- Having a firearm concealed carry permit
- Owning a business
- Being a registered voter and actively voting
- Being a taxpayer
- Being active in your community

Life Lesson 35

Two areas in your home to invest your money in: (1) your bathroom(s) and (2) your kitchen(s).

Life Lesson 36

Never compromise your integrity.

Life Lesson 37

Never compromise your credit rating for anyone.

Life Lesson 38

Good credit is like oxygen; you absolutely need it.

Life Lesson 39

Date women who like you, but marry the woman who believes, trust, and respects you.

Life Lesson 40

If you make a contract, your word and your signature are worth the same thing.

Life Lesson 41

If you're the smartest person in your circle, then your circle is the wrong one to be in.

Life Lesson 42

Do business and keep relationships with people that have the same values as yours.

Life Lesson 43

Arguing and arguments are for emotionally weak-minded people.

Life Lesson 44

Sometimes doing something good causes a negative result.

Life Lesson 45

Life formula: Sacrifice your time to make life-changing money, then take the money to create unlimited time. Time = Money = Time.

Life Lesson 46

Stay physically fit, mentally sound, and spiritually grounded.

Life Lesson 47

No matter how much money you make, you can only wear one pair of shoes, drive one car, or live in one home at one time.

Life Lesson 48

Never circumvent the process of anything you are trying to accomplish.

Life Lesson 49

Always respect your life because you only get one.

Life Lesson 50

Never date the ex-girlfriend, side chick, fiancé, or ex-wife of your friend, coworker, associate, or family member.

The Final Lesson

Everything we do has a specific purpose in our timeline. Everything we encounter—good or bad, compassionate or horrendous—has a purpose and a meaning for our personal journey. Everything cannot be explained, and sometimes it's as simple as just asking an ABC type of question. No journey has pathways filled with honey. Struggle and opposition strengthen your steel so that you may always fight the good fight of life with the sword of God in your hands. Let's look at some final examples of how not seeing the writing on the wall can be our greatest mistake.

Giants can fall and why they do—ten businesses too big to fail that totally flopped

10. *Kodak.* Created in 1888, they developed the first digital film camera in 1975. Filed for bankruptcy in 2012. They failed to adjust to the smartphone camera and GoPro wave.

9. *Xerox.* Launched the first commercial copy machine in 1959. The company did over $500 million dollars in revenue in 1965. Concepts designed by Xerox employees were *given* away to Apple and Microsoft at *no cost* by Xerox employees. Apple and Microsoft developed and marketed these technologies to consumers and the world. Not too smart of Xerox.

8. *Polaroid.* Founded in 1937, it was most popular in the 1990s, hitting the company's peak in 1991. In 2001 the company filed for bankruptcy.

7. *Yahoo.* In 2016 they were the sixth most visited website in the world. In 2011 it was the third largest email provider in the world. In 2002 they had a deal to buy Google. They passed on buying them. Then in 2006 they had a deal to buy Facebook, and they passed on this deal as well.

6. *MySpace.* Founded in 2003, they were first social network platform. In 2006 it was the most visited website in the world. It was purchased in 2005 by News Corporation and in 2011 by Time.

5. *Sears.* Founded in Illinois in the late nineteenth century. From 1969 to 1989, it was the largest retailer in the United States. In 2018 it had 182 stores compared to the 3,500 it had in 2008. Walmart took a strategic approach and eventually pushed Sears out of business.

4. *BlackBerry.* Founded in 1984, it was one of the first major smartphones. The company sold fifty million units in 2011. They once controlled 50 percent of the smartphone market. The lack of change from keyboard to touchscreen did the company in.

3. *Blockbuster.* It once had over nine thousand stores at one time. In 2000 Netflix offered Blockbuster the opportunity to

purchase their company for fifty million dollars. Blockbuster passed on the deal.

2. *Borders.* Founded in 1971, 70 percent of their stores were competing with Barnes and Noble. They owed $350 million in debt.

1. *Toys R Us.* In the late 1990s they were largest toy retailer. They signed a ten-year deal with Amazon in 2000. Amazon started selling their own toys which caused the company's demise. Damn.

In conclusion, I would tell you to trust few and help many. Plan and replan. Dream big and work smart. Execute better than most and stay focused. The path to greatness is always based on our choices. I made the best choice when I became a father. With love and always love, Dad.

> To beat me he's gonna have to kill me, to kill me he's gonna have to stand in front me, and to stand in front of me he's gonna have to have the heart to do that. (Sylvester Stallone, *Rocky IV*)

For all the Hoop Dream kids in New York

NCAA division 1 men's basketball programs

- Syracuse University—Syracuse, New York
- Stony Brook University—Stony Brook, New York
- Colgate University—Hamilton, New York
- St. Bonaventure—Saint Bonaventure, New York
- Hofstra University—Hempstead, New York
- Fordham University—Bronx, New York
- Buffalo University—Buffalo, New York
- Siena College—Loudonville, New York
- Wagner College—Staten Island, New York
- St. John's University—Queens, New York
- Columbia University—Manhattan, New York

- Canisius College—Buffalo, New York
- Albany University—Albany, New York
- Cornell University—Ithaca, New York
- Binghamton University—Vestal, New York
- Iona College—New Rochelle, New York
- Marist College—Poughkeepsie, New York
- Manhattan College—Bronx, New York
- Niagara University—Lewiston, New York
- St. Francis College—Brooklyn, New York

My youngest son, Chase, was the initial inspiration for this book. He and my older son, Sean, play and played AAU basketball as well as CYO, middle and high school basketball. Every young child, male or female, who plays the game of basketball at a competitive level would love to make the NBA or the WNBA. College basketball is a part of that journey. New York has twenty men's division 1 programs that the young men of my state should investigate. Happy hooping, gentlemen.

Sources

Chapter 1

- Henry Wadsworth Longfellow, hard work, quote.
- Life Lesson 1—*patience* and *self-control*, Dr. Rupert N. Green; definition by Merriam-Webster.
- Life Lesson 3—*pride*, definition by Merriam-Webster.
- Life Lesson 6—Juelz Santana Drink Champs interview via YouTube, June 4, 2022.
- Life Lesson 7—the Bible, book of Proverbs 22:7, New Living Translation version.
- Life Lesson 20—Ramon Rivera and Khoury Porter.
- All other lessons—Khoury Porter.

Chapter 2

- Money personalities, A. MacArthur Barr Middle School.
- *Credit* definition, Oxford Dictionary.
- *Credit worthiness* definition, Rajeev Dhir, April 5, 2021 (www.investopedia.com).
- *Credit score* definition, October 17, 2022 (www.consumerfinance.gov).
- FICO versus VantageScore (five differences) (www.usatoday.com) and personal finance, Barry Paperno (www.credit.com), December 21, 2017, 4:00 p.m.
- *Cryptocurrency* definition, crypto basics: what is cryptocurrency? (www.coinbase.com).
- Most popular cryptocurrencies—cryptocurrency basics: what is cryptocurrency? (www.coinbase.com).
- Cryptocurrency information (www.coinbase.com).

- Crypto history—Bitcoin (www.money.usnews.com), "The History of Bitcoin, the First Cryptocurrency," Wayne Duggan, August 31, 2022. Ethereum (www.bernardmarr. com). Blockchain: A Very Short History of Ethereum Everyone Should read. Litecoin—Litecoin (LTC) by Jake Frankenfield, updated March 25, 2022 (www.investope-dia.com). Bitcoin Cash- by Jake Frankenfield, updated October 4, 2022 (www.investopedia.com). Ripple by Jake Frankenfield, updated October 4, 2022, cryptocur-rency/Alt coins (www.investopedia.com). Iota by Jake Frankenfield, updated August 27, 2021, cryptocurrency / Strategy and Education (www.investopedia.com). Tether by Jake Frankenfield, updated May 12, 2022, cryptocur-rency/Alt coins (www.investopedia.com).
- NFT—What is an NFT? Non-Fungible Tokens explained by Robyn Conti, John Schimdt, Benjamin Curry, updated April 8, 2022 (www.forbes.com).
- How Much Money Do I Keep—Federal Income Tax (mar-ried) 2021–2022 tax brackets and federal income tax rates (www.turbotax.intuit.com). NYS tax rate (www.nerdwal-let.com). New York State income tax: Rates and Who Pays in 2022 written by Tina Orem, September 1, 2022 (mar-ried filing jointly).
- Social security and Medicare tax rates (www.ssa.gov).
- *Residual income* definition, Ellis Burgin, February 4, 2020, updated May 10, 2020 (www.indeed.com).
- *Personal residual income* definition, Ellis Burgin, February 4, 2020 (www.indeed.com).
- Residual income formula by Ellis Burgin, February 4, 2020 (www.indeed.com).
- Passive income by Ellis Burgin, February 4, 2020 (www. indeed.com).
- Types of residual income by Ellis, February 4, 2020 (www. indeed.com).
- 1 Timothy 6:9–10, the Bible, New Living Translation.

- Personal residual income, residual income formula, passive income, types of residual income, "What Is Residual Income?" Definition and Types by Ellis Burgin, updated May 10, 2022, and published February 4, 2020 (www.indeed.com).

Chapter 3

- Kenneth Chenault. Business leaders/CEOs. Who Is Kenneth I. Chenault? By Lucas Downey, updated January 2, 2022 (www.investopedia.com).
- (Byron Allen (www.wikipedia.com).
- Marvin Ellison (www.celebritynetworth.com).
- Kenneth Frazier. Meet The Richest Black CEOs of Fortune 500 companies in America 2021 by Bernadette Giacomazzo, September 3, 2021 (www.afrotech.com).
- Rene F. Jones. M&T C.E.O Rene' Jones' compensation reaches $4.77 million by Matt Glynn, March 7, 2019 (www.buffalonews.com). Rene Jones Net Worth, last updated October 25, 2022, at 7:42 p.m. EST (www.wallmine.com).
- Inventions by African Americans (www.dailyhive.com). 120 Things You Probably Didn't Know were created by Black Inventors by Alyssa Therrien February 4, 2021, 3:48 p.m. Philip B. Downing—the mailbox. Alexander Miles—automatic elevator doors. Joseph H. Smith—lawn sprinkler. George T. Sampson—clothes dryer 1892. Patricia Bath—the laserphaco probe. (www.biography.com) April 2, 2014. William H. Richardson (www.1011now.com). Telling the Untold by Kamri Sylve, February 9, 2021, 8:57 a.m. CST. Osbourn Dorsey (www.theoptionalfacts.com and www.thougtco.com). Lewis Latimer- (www.nsucurrent.nova.edu). Black Inventors, February 25, 2015, by: Destinee Hughes. Thomas Marshall—fire extinguisher sprinkler system 1872. Nathaniel Alexander by Mary Bellis updated on July 28, 2019 (thoughtco.com). www.pga.com by Bob Denney published February 10, 2018; How Dr. George F. Grant went

from African American dentist to golf tee inventor. Robert F. Fleming Jr (www.wikipedia.org). The First Lock Improvement is patented; Washington A. Martin 1889 patented the lock (www.aaregistry.org). Elijah Mc Coy (www.invent.org). 1872 is the correct date. George Washington Carver (www.legalzoom.com) and Honoring George Washington Carver by Heleigh Bostwick, updated May 2, 2022 (300 patents) all peanut products. John Love (www.biography.com) original published April 2, 2014, updated June 1, 2020. Edmond Berger (www.automotivehistory.org) published February 2, 2022, by Thomas A. Carrington. Charles Brooks (www.myblackhistory.net) correction 1896. Fredrick M. Jones—automatic refrigeration system (www.aaregistry.org, reference www.msthalloffame.org). Garrett Morgan (www.thoughtco.com) by Mary Bellis, updated on November 24, 2019. AB Blackburn (www.interestingengineering.com) A-Z list of Black and African American inventors and inventions by Christopher McFadden, July 13, 2018, 5:24 a.m. JA Burr (www.thoughtco.com) biography of John Albert Burr by Mary Bellis updated October 2, 2019. Sources Ikenson, Ben "Patents": Ingenious Inventions How They Work and How They Came to Be" Running Press, 2012 Ngeow, Evelyn, ed "Inventors and Inventions, volume 1 "New York": Marshall Cavendish 2008. O. E. Brown by (www.lotepiolaw.com) June 29, 2012, Buffalo Inventor: Oscar E. Brown—Now that's a "horseshoe" of a different color! G.F. Grant (www.pga.com), How Dr. George F. Grant went from African American dentist to golf tee inventor by Bob Denney published on Saturday, February 10, 2018. Joseph H. Dickinson (www.thoughtco.com) Biography of Musical Inventor Joseph H Dickinson by Mary Bellis, updated on June 13, 2019.

- The richest man in the history of the world—Mansa Musa: the African king who was the richest man in history (www.history.co.uk).
- How '64 helped millions. Legal Highlight: The Civil Rights Act of 1964 US Department of Labor. Office of

the Assistant Secretary for Administration of Management (www.dol.gov).

- The roar of the panther (www.history.com). How The Black Panthers Breakfast Program Both Inspired and Threatened the Government By: Erin Blakemore January 29, 2021 updated original: February 6, 2018. (www.time.com) With Free Medical Clinics and Patient Advocacy, the Black Panthers Created a Legacy in Community Health That Still Exists Amid Covid-19 by Olivia B. Waxman, February 25, 2021, 12:08 p.m. EST.
- Hip-hop music and culture by: Greg Tate, last updated December 5, 2022 (www.britannica.com).
- Jazz music—Smithsonian Jazz/Education (www.american-history.si.edu).
- Rhythm and blues music (www.loc.gov).
- Rock and roll music by Greg Kot, last updated December 9, 2022 (www.britannica.com).
- Gospel music by Virginia Gorlinski (www.britannica.com).
- Jack Daniels Whiskey—The Secret History of the Slave Behind Jack Daniel's Whiskey, January 28, 2019 (www.gastropod.com).
- The moon walk dance—Little Known Black History Fact: The First Moonwalk D. L. Chandler (www.blackamericaweb.com),
- The high five hand gesture— by S. M. Mamunur Rahman, March 20, 2021, "A Brief History of High Five" (www.medium.com).
- The American Cowboy—Cowboys by history.com editors, updated October 10, 2019, original: April 26, 2010 (www.history.com).
- The Buffalo Soldiers—Buffalo Soldiers by history.com editors, updated January 25, 2021, original December 7, 2017 (www.history.com).
- The Afro hairstyle by Chime Edwards, updated October 27, 2020. The Impact of the Fro in The Civil Rights Movement (www.essence.com).

- The hustle and electric slide dances (www.arthurmurrayraleigh.com). Hustle (learn all about the hustle) (www.afro.com). It's Electric: A little slide before we go by Micha Green June 20, 2021.
- Tap and jazz dance (www.loc.gov). Tap Dance in America A Short History by: Constance V. Hill (www.britiannica.com). Jazz dance by the editors of Encyclopedia Britannica.
- Perm hairstyle. A History of the Perm Hairstyle, published March 26, 2018 (www.glamourdaze.com).
- Urban based American slang (www.americanheritage.com). Slang by Hugh Rawson October 2003, volume 54, issue 5.
- Beef patty—"The Beef Patty is Jamaica in the Palm of your Hand" by Bryan Washington, February 23, 2022 (www.nytimes.com).
- Rice—How rice shaped the American South by Michael W. Twitty, March 8, 2021 (www.bbc.com).
- Capitalism—The Clear Connection Between Slavery and American Capitalism by Dina Gerdeman, May 3, 2017, 12:47 p.m. EDT (www.forbes.com).
- Red Lining by Becky Little, October 20, 2020. How a New Deal Housing Program Enforced Segregation (www.history.com).
- Gentrification—resource library. Grades 5–8 subjects' anthropology social studies, sociology, US history (www.education.nationalgeographic.org).
- Capitalism (www.merriam-webster.com).
- Capitalize (www.merriam-webster.com).
- Examples of capitalization—Dirty Little Secrets About Black History, Its Heroes, and Other Troublemakers by: Claud Anderson ED. D chapter 6 pg. 83 Slavery Gave Birth to Capitalism. Stamp, Kenneth the Peculiar Institution (New York: Vintage Books) 1956 and John Ashworth. Slavery, Capitalism and Politics in the Antebellum Republic. (Mass: Cambridge Up) 1995. Celebrity Real Estate, August 24, 2022, by Zach Schiffman. Neil Patrick Harris Just Sold the Priciest Townhouse in Harlem (www.

curbed.com). The Harlem Brownst, December 22, 2020 (www.brownstonedetectives.com). City to Sell 13 lots in Harlem for Housing, at $1 a piece by Nina Siegal, August 30, 2000 (www.nytimes.com).

- Henrietta Lacks (www.en.m.wikipedia.org).
- Mana Musa. This 14th Century African Emperor Remains the Richest Person in History by Thaddeus Morgan, March 19, 2018 (www.history.com).
- Ramesses 2 by Peter F. Dorman, last updated October 25, 2020 (www.britannica.com).
- Hannibal—Who was Hannibal? by Kristin Baird Rattini, March 4, 2019 (www.nationalgeographic.com).
- Shaka Zulu by: Donald R. Morris, last updated November 25, 2022 (www.britannica.com).
- Nelson Mandela, published April 27, 2017, updated January 6, 2021 (www.biography.com).
- Martin Luther King Jr by history.com editors, updated January 11, 2022, original November 9, 2009 (www.history.com).
- Malcolm X by history.com editors, updated November 2, 2022, original October 29, 2009 (www.history.com).
- Huey P. Newton and Bobby Seale by the editors of encyclopedia Britannica, updated December 5, 2022, and October 18, 2022 (www.britannica.com).
- Josiah Henson by Jared Brock, May 16, 2018, The Story of Josiah Henson the Real Inspiration for "Uncle Toms Cabin" (www.smithsonianmag.com).
- Barak Obama (www.whitehouse.gov)
- Muhammad Ali by Thomas Hauser, last updated November 30, 2022 (www.britannica.com).
- Walter Lincoln Hawkins (www.aaregistry.org)

Chapter 4

- *Sacrifice* definition (www.merriam-webster.com).
- *Commitment* definition (www.merriam-webster.com).

- *Focus* definition (www.merriam-webster.com).
- *Discipline* definition (www.merriam-webster.com).
- Habit (www.merriam-webster.com).
- Self-employed—"What Is Self-Employment?" by Maya Dollarhide, updated April 29, 2022 (www.investopedia.com).
- Business owner—What is a Business Owner? (www.accountingcourse.com).
- Types of businesses—choose a business structure (www.sba.gov).
- Warren Buffett. Warren Buffet bought a pinball machine for $25 in 1946 and started the best business I was ever in (www.cnbc.com). 22 Mind-Blowing Facts about Warren Buffett and his wealth. 4 Reasons Warren Buffett's American Express Investment was Genius (www.moneyminiblog.com).
- Sam Walton biography—everything to know about the Walmart founder (www.entrepreneur.com).
- Michael Dell by the editors of Encyclopedia Britannica, September 6, 2007 (www.britannica.com).
- William Gates III, aka Bill Gates, American computer programmer, businessman, and philanthropist, by the editors of Encyclopedia Britannica, July 20, 1998, last updated October 24, 2022 (www.britannica.com).
- 3 stages of business—what does "In the Black or "In the Red" mean? (www.skynova.com) and Khoury Porter
- 5 lessons on building stronger networks. "Your Network Is Your Net worth: 5 Lessons on Building Stronger Networks" by Alp Mimaroglu, February 2, 2018 (www.entrepreneur.com).
- Business that are recession and pandemic proof—Khoury Porter and Businesses to start during a recession by Legal Zoom, updated December 5, 2022 (www.legalzoom.com).
- *Failure* definition (www.merriam-webster.com).
- Businesses with the lowest failure, highest failure, and failure percentages—What Percentage of Businesses Fail in the

First Year? (Plus, Top Causes of Business Failure), October 21, 2022 (www.freshbooks.com).

- *Self-employed* definition—Article: "What Is Self-Employment?" by Maya Dollarhide Reviewed by Margaret James, updated April 29, 2022.

Chapter 5

- The lifeboat by Khoury Porter
- The four types of liar—an illustrated guide to the four types of liars (www.nirandfar.com).
- Stock market statistics, facts, and history—"Top 25 Incredible Stock Market Statistics and Facts in 2022" by G. Dautovic, updated December 16, 2022 (www.fortunaly.com).

Chapter 6

- *Religion* definition (www.merriam-webster.com).
- Judaism by history.com editors, January 5, 2018 (www.history.com).
- Christianity by history.com editors, October 13, 2017 (www.history.com).
- Islam by history.com editors, January 5, 2018 (www.history.com).
- Buddhism by history.com editors, October 12, 2017 (www.history.com).
- Twenty life skills not taught in school by Jake Akins, updated November 22, 2022 (www.successfulstudent.org).
- What we learn in school (K-5)—"A Guide to What Your Child Will Learn by Grade" by Amanda Morin, updated on July 8, 2021, fact-checked by Rich Scherr (www.verywellfamily.com).
- Middle school. "Top skills middle school students need to thrive, and how parents can help" by Phyllis L. Fagell, February 29, 2016 (www.washingtonpostcom).

- Highschool. Why High School is Important and How to Make the most of it (www.beta-bowl.com).
- Colleges and universities. What's the difference between college and a university? (www.mydegreeguide.com).
- *University* definition (www.mydegreeguide.com).
- College and university stats and facts—"10 Facts about Today's college graduates" by Katherine Schaeffer, April 12, 2022 (www.pewresearch.org).

Chapter 7

- "How Does a College Degree Improve a Graduates' Earning and Employment" (www.aplu.org).
- "Lifetime Earnings by Level of Education" (www.aplu.org).
- 25 Highest Paid Occupations in the U.S. by Jim Probasco, updated November 20, 2022, reviewed by Doretha Clemon, fact-checked by Vikki Velasquez (www.ivestopedia.com).
- 32 Jobs That Pay $100k without an Advanced Degree by publisher, last updated August 11, 2022 (www.trade-schools.net).

Chapter 8

- *Felony* definition (www.google.com, Oxford languages).
- *Misdemeanor* definition—Khoury R. Porter.
- *Violations* definition (www.lawinsider.com, violation of law).
- *Criminal charge* definition (www.en.m.wikipedia.org, criminal charge article).
- *Probation* definition (www.enwikipediaorg, probation article).
- Types of felonies and misdemeanors list—Khoury Porter.
- Felony classes and sentence guidelines in NYS (www. New-york-lawyers.org, sentencing guideline for non-drug felonies).

- Misdemeanor classes and sentence guidelines in NYS (www.new-york-lawyers.org, sentencing guidelines for misdemeanors and violations)
- Miranda Rights—"Know your rights: What Are Miranda Rights?" by Stephanie Morrow, updated July 27, 2022 (www.legalzoom.com).
- The Bill of Rights of The United States (www.archives.gov, America's Founding Documents). The Bill of Rights: A Transcription.
- Supreme Court cases that changed America (www.uscourts. gov, Supreme Court Landmarks).

Chapter 9

- Thirty-six shocking statistics on fatherless homes (www. lifeisbeautiful.org, statistics section, "36 Shocking Statistics on Fatherless Homes," October 4, 2018).

Chapter 10

- The three pillars of health—Khoury Porter.
- Anxiety disorders to schizophrenia (www.betterhealth.vic. gov.au, mental health services; types of mental health issues and illness).
- The human body and our health—*The Book of Unusual Knowledge* by Publications International, Ltd April 1, 2012 (published) pg. 604.
- Twelve activities to burn calories and fat—*The Book of Unusual Knowledge* by Publications International, Ltd April 1, 2012, pgs. 594–595.
- The difference between fruits and veggies—*Why Does Popcorn Pop* by Don Vorhees, pg. 25.
- The difference between herbs and spices, pg. 121.
- Different types of drinking, pgs. 156–157.
- Vitamins—"the big thirteen" (www.readersdigest.ca, updated January 6, 2022).

- How People Learn—United States Concealed Carry Association Instructor training course 2020 (summer).
- Spinach information—*Why Does Popcorn Pop* by Don Vorhees, pg. 43.

Chapter 11

- According to Einstein (www.goodreads.com, Albert Einstein quotes).
- Words of Malcom—"A Man Who Stands for Nothing Will Fall Anything—Here are 150 Best Malcolm X quotes" by Sagine Corrielus, February 11, 2021 (www.parade.com).
- What do I need to start my own business? by Khoury Porter.
- Types of retirement plans (www.irs.gov).
- Life insurance—why you need it. "5 Top Benefits of life insurance" by Kat Tretina, updated February 26, 2022 (www.investopedia.com).
- What is a trust fund? "Wealth, Trust, and Estate Planning. What Is a trust fund and How Does It Work?" by Akhilesh Ganti, updated July 7, 2022, reviewed by: Ebony Howard, fact-checked by Ryan Eichler (www.investopedia.com).
- Annuities by Dylan Huang/Senior Vice President and head of retirement and wealth management solutions. What are different types of annuities? (www.newyorklife.com).

Chapter 12

- Homeownership—"The Top 10 Benefits of Homeownership: Why You Should Buy a Home" (www.helenpainter.com)
- Giants Can Fall and Why They Do by Adrian Sharp, fact-checked by Rachel Jones. 10 Businesses Too Big to Fail That Totally Flopped (www.listverse.com, miscellaneous January 3, 2022).
- NCAA Division 1 Men's basketball—2021 Top New York men's D1 basketball schools (www.collegefactual.com).

About the Author

Born in the Bronx, New York, the author grew up in the Edenwald section of the Bronx, then he moved to the southside of Yonkers, New York, and remained there until 2006. He was a Westchester County correctional officer for seven years and has been an Orangetown police officer for the past five years. He is a black belt in three different systems of martial arts, as well as a professional and amateur boxing coach. He owns Hudson Valley Martial Arts and Boxing in Congers, New York, and he is a part owner of North Bergen Mixed Martial Arts and Boxing in North Bergen, New Jersey. He also owns and operates SRP Tactical, a firearms training and consulting school, and he is part owner of RPS Solution LLC, an NYS security guard and executive protection company.